The Monongahela

RIVERS OF AMERICA BOOKS

ALREADY PUBLISHED ARE:

RIVERS OF AMERICA

Edited by

Carl Carmer

As planned and started by

Constance Lindsay Skinner

Associate Editor **Jean Crawford**

Art Editor **Benjamin Feder**

THE
MONONGAHELA

by
RICHARD BISSELL

Illustrated by
John O'Hara Cosgrave II

Rinehart & Co., Inc.

New York

Toronto

Grateful acknowledgment is made to Louis C. Hunter, of the Industrial College of the Armed Forces in Washington, D.C., for permission to use excerpts from *Steamboats on the Western Rivers;* to Vanguard Press, Inc., New York, N.Y., for permission to quote brief excerpts from *Incredible Carnegie* by John K. Winkler; and to Bernard De Voto for excerpts from an article in *Harper's Magazine*.

PUBLISHED   SIMULTANEOUSLY   IN   CANADA
BY CLARKE, IRWIN & COMPANY, LTD., TORONTO

LIBRARY OF CONGRESS CATALOG CARD NUMBER:—52-5562

TO CURLY AND IRONJAW AND CRAZY MIKE,
FELLOW PILOTS ON THE OLD MON.

Contents

List of Illustrations

Monongahela River

The Monongahela River is formed by the confluence of the West Fork and Tygart Rivers about 1 mile south of Fairmont, West Virginia. It flows in a northeasterly direction into southwestern Pennsylvania and then in a northerly direction to Pittsburgh, Pennsylvania, where it joins the Allegheny to form the Ohio River. Total length of the river is about 128 miles, of which 127.7 are marked with daymarks, 119 miles are buoyed, and 117.2 miles are lighted by navigation lights.

DISTRICT ENGINEER
PITTSBURGH DISTRICT
CORPS OF ENGINEERS, U.S. ARMY
PITTSBURGH, PA.
JANUARY, 1951

The Monongahela

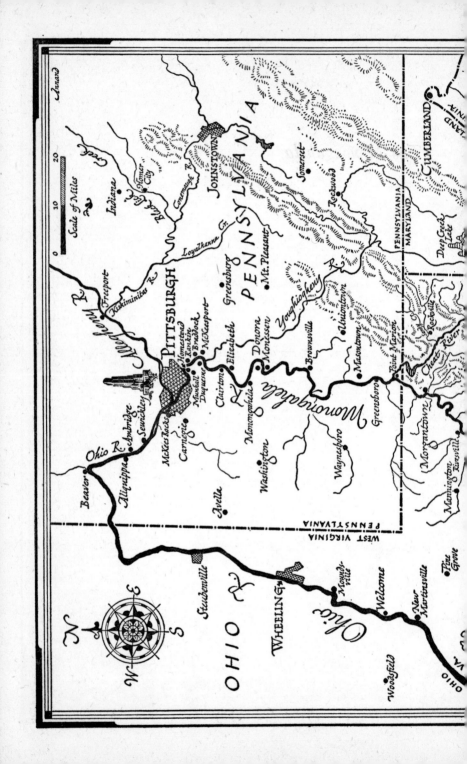

The
Monongahela

The "Coal Queen"

I plugged up and down the Illinois River for a couple of years as deckhand on the towboats, hauling coal from Havana up to Joliet, and then in the drainage canal up to Chicago, and the draft board took the second mate, so Captain Bloodworth called me up to the pilothouse and said, "You're the new second mate." I took my paper suitcase out of the pigpen and up to the mates' room, and one thing sure, that mates' room smelled better than the deckhands' bunkroom, and even had a light in the bunk to read by, and a clean blanket with no fuel oil or coal ground into it. You go out and carry ratchets and chains and those 100-foot lock lines for a while and you will understand what I felt like to be a mate. I couldn't have felt any better if they'd made me governor of the state.

I was mate there for over a year. We brought up a lot of coal from down below, and if summer nights in the canal weren't much of a treat to the nose, and winter nights pulling ice cakes out of the lock gates weren't very romantic, still it was $145 a month and all you could eat, and ten days off with pay every forty, a good tavern near the dock at Joliet, and the boat was a home.

One afternoon a week or so before Thanksgiving

when the wind from Lake Michigan was slicing down through the frame houses and factories, we had just tied off six loads at the Joliet landing and the shore watchman came hunting me up where I was having coffee in the galley.

"Ole Murphy he wants to see you up in the office," he said. "My, I wisht I was a big mate so's I could set in the galley drinkin' coffee."

"You wanna make this trip downriver and back for me?" I said.

"I gotta get back," he said.

I went up to the office and Helen, the new office girl with the glasses, told me to go right in, that Captain Murphy was waiting for me.

"Not that I think you'll ever amount to a damn," says Murphy looking out the window at the canal with a sour look, "but the pilot on the *Coal Queen* fell off a barge last night and got himself drownded like a jackass and the boat is tied up. Now you go and pack up and take the train for Morgantown—you can be there tomorrow afternoon."

"Okay," I said, feeling a little dizzy. "But I'm no pilot, and where in hell is Morgantown? I never heard of it."

"West Virginia," he said. "Monongahela River. You stand a few watches and you'll either be a pilot or in the nuthouse. Now get goin'. Expense money from Miss Rundel."

"I never knew the company had boats way over there," I said.

"There's a lot of other things you don't know," he said, "but don't let the strain injure your brains."

A couple of days later, after missing a train in Pittsburgh and other incidents, I got off a crummy old day coach and there I was in Morgantown, and a guy comes up and says, "Are you Bissell?"

"Yes, I am, and where is the boat?"

He loaded me in his car and said we would go out to the landing and I could go to work right away, they had only been doing day work since the pilot drowned—the captain was working days and they tied up nights.

We came down across some tracks toward the Monongahela and I noticed a little old dirty boat with a telescoping pilothouse and a single stack, a piece of marine junk overdue for the scrap yard.

"Who owns that palatial yacht?" I said.

"Why, that's the *Coal Queen*," he said. "That's the boat."

"Uh-huh," I said. "Well, let's you and me go right down to the depot again. I can probably still get a train out this afternoon."

"Why," says the shore boss, looking hurt, "what's the matter?"

"Why, man oh man, I just came off the *Inland Coal*, 1,350 horsepower Atlas Imperial. What makes you think I'm gonna live in this old converted oil drum?" I said. "Look at the stack, tied up there with baling wire. Look at that deck—looks like Blum's junk yard. Look at them tow knees all bunged over. And what are them two dwarfs standin' there all over coal dust? Deckhands, I suppose, or is that the captain and chief engineer?"

Well, I went aboard. What the hell, it was awfully cold back on the Illinois. I pretty near changed my mind again once I got aboard though. What a layout. First place, all the officers, the deckhands, and the cook slept in one bunkroom in a great pile of bunks, suitcases, pillows with no pillowcases, shoes, overalls, comic books, oily blankets, newspapers, shaving cream, oilskins, dirty socks, orange peel, cigarette butts, coffee cups, underwear, rubber boots, foot powder, razors, *Western Stories*, and cough syrup. And in order to get the most benefit out of all this, the system was to keep all the windows sealed tight and get an oil-soaked engineer and a couple of ripe deckhands in there, get the cook to fire up his pipe with some Plough Boy, turn the stove up high, and leave the whole thing to simmer for six hours at a time.

I opened the door and went in the bunkroom. A slim, swarthy-looking bird with curly hair and sheik mustache was lying on a bunk reading *Blue Beetle Comics* and smoking cigarettes; he had his shirt off and his shoes off and his feet resting politely on the pillow of the next bunk.

"Ain't this here Blue Beetle the goddamnedest?" he said to me as I set down my case and lit a Revelation to kill some of the smell.

"They sent me over here to go pilot," I said. "Where's the captain at?"

"What a shame," he answered. "Now we got to go to work again. My, it's been peaceful here since Happy drownded."

FIGURE I. THE *Coal Queen*.

"You the captain?" I asked.

"I'm it," he said. "Ain't it the berries? What boat you come off of?"

"The *Inland Coal*," I said.

"Finding it kind of a shock so far, hey, buddy?" he said. He got up and stretched, and reached over and poked some old boy asleep in a bunk across from him and hollered, "Gas! Get the hell outa there. Here's the new pilot aboard and that's his bunk from now on. Come on, Gas, you'll hafta double up with National."

This deckhand was in between the sheets in his work clothes—an old pair of greasy pants and check wool shirt —and even had his shoes on. You can imagine what a deckhand's shoes have to put up with in the way of oil, coal dust, water, mud, grease, and paint in a six-hour watch, so you can picture the sheets easily enough. He rolled out and fell on another bunk about four feet away.

"Where'd that guy get a name like Gas?" I said.

"Come on up to the pilothouse," says the captain. "Why, that's because he comes from Edna Gas."

"Maybe I better go home," I said. "What's Edna Gas?"

"Why, man, it's one of these here coal mines upriver a ways. That's his home. His ole man is blacksmith at the mine."

We got up in the pilothouse. There was just barely room for the two of us, quite a change from the big roomy pilothouses I was used to, with benches, chairs, stoves, water coolers, and so on.

"Hey, National," the captain hollered, sliding the windows back. "Get up off yer dead ass and turn that line loose. Come on, buddy, let's go!" And one of the dwarfs, who had been sitting on the bank looking at his shoelaces, got up and commenced to turn her loose.

"Where's he come from?" I asked.

"National Consolidated, up by Lock 14."

"Why don't you call him Consolidated, then?"

"Sometimes we do." He gave the engineer a backing

bell, and the old Fairbanks-Morse shot a bushel basket of soot and rust out the stack, which was right behind the pilothouse, and the boat commenced backing away from the bank into the stream.

"Hey, National," he hollered down to the deck, "bring us up a couple coffees, okay?"

"Where we goin'?" I said.

"We're goin' over to the Dupont landing and pick up an empty and take off for Kingmont. You watch me make the pickup and this first lock and then you can take her."

"Okay, but understand this is all new to me. I never piloted anything bigger'n a Illinois River duckboat."

"Didn't you never steer on the *Inland* and them other boats?"

"Why, sure, but any damn fool can steer out in the river. It's these here locks and landings makes it hard."

"Aw, have some coffee. It ain't bad."

We got across the river and there was a fleet of about ten or fifteen barges, empties and loads, and a big coalyard behind them. And then piled up on the hill behind the heaps of coal was the damnedest-looking plant you ever saw, a monster—big buildings and towers, chimneys and trestles, cranes and sheds, smoke, flames, cinders. I don't know what they made there but they called it the Morgantown Ordnance and we expected to see the whole works blow up most any time and move Monongalia County down around Pittsburgh someplace.

We came up on the barge fleet and the captain rang a slow bell and then a stopping bell and we drifted up easy to an empty barge.

"What's your name?" the captain asked me.

"Bissell," I said.

"Okay, Beedle, now watch how we face up to this here empty," and he never called me anything else again as long as I knew him except when he wanted to borrow money, and then he used my first name.

The deckhand got up on the deck of the empty and grabbed the face wires and dumped them in place on the timberheads. Then he trotted out to the other end of the barge and turned it loose, and before we even had the wires tightened up the captain gave a full ahead bell and we bounced alongside a couple of empties, cleared them, and sailed off up the river. The whole thing didn't take more than three or four minutes.

"My God, do you make all your landings that fast?" I asked.

"Beedle, we make 'em as fast as we can, boy," he said.

"How much coal do we deliver there?"

"All we can tow," he said. "We gave 'em 68,000 tons last month. Here, get the feel of this here thing," and he got up off the pilot's chair. "Set down, Beedle, and make yourself at home. I'm goin' down and get me a slice of salami. Just hold her off this point easy and the lock is around the bend."

"If you say so," I said.

"Call me Duke," and he climbed down the ladder to the deck.

It was a dreary day for sure, with a greasy sky, and a yellowish foggy smoke hanging in the air, and the whole world looked sick and sad. The damned old barge in front of me was a cheerless, banged-up derelict, I was 900 miles from home and still had a hangover from my stopover in Pittsburgh, and I was very lonesome for Joliet and those familiar locks and landings—Dresden Island, Starved Rock, Brandon Road, and the canal into Chicago. I couldn't see myself sleeping down there in that rat's nest, even to be a pilot. However, the sensation of being at last a pilot, even on this tin can, grew increasingly pleasant, and I lit a cigarette, leaned back on the pilot's stool, and steered with my feet.

The door opened and National stuck his head in. "Say, cap, you want some more coffee?"

That was the first time anybody ever called me "cap," and it sounded pretty fair after I had been crawling around on deck so long with my ears full of soft coal.

"No, no more coffee now," I said. "Say, where's that lock at?"

"You'll see it in a minute. You can blow for it any time now."

Sure enough, out of the yellow winter fog I saw the lock and I found the whistle and blew a long and a short. Duke showed up with a pile of crackers with salami in between them.

"No, I'll take you in, Beedle, and show you how we do it over here. Want some salami?" He gave me a handful.

Man, I never saw anything like the way we went into that lock. We slammed into her like a taxicab on Wabash Avenue about 5:00 P.M. And when they had raised the water and opened the upper gate we came charging out with the barge alongside, turned it loose, picked it up again on the fly, knocked some concrete off the lock wall with our stern, and away we flew like a wild mustang.

"National," Duke shouted down to the deck, "bring up a couple more coffees."

So I took her again and Duke went down and tackled *Blue Beetle*. This was the toughest, dreariest, most godforsaken-looking country I ever saw—the hills looked as though a battle had just been fought among the barren trees; they were desolate, dirty, scarred, and under the dull winter sky looked like there was not much hope left anyplace.

The mines, with their coal tipples and lines of coal cars, and the clusters of unpainted frame company houses, and slate piles and muddy streets and Royal Crown Cola signs, made you sick just to look at them. How a man could put in his time whacking away underground and come out into a mess like this and raise up a family in one of these terrible-looking shanties was more than I could understand. It was just homesickness working on me, I suppose—God knows there are some awful places along the drainage canal and in South Chicago, places that would give you the blues even on a spring morning.

Later on I got used to the burnt-over look to things, and it seemed natural and right to me that the world should consist of coal mines, coal trains, coal houses, coal taverns, coal trees, coal streets, coal children, coal everything.

This was bad enough on this dismal afternoon, but

night came, and I had some pot roast and apple pie in the galley-messroom, a little hole aft of the engine room, and Duke said, "You lay down and I'll call you at midnight. Get some sleep, Beedle."

I lay down and tossed around for a couple of hours, dozed, woke up, heard shouts out on deck, dozed, woke, listened to National snoring, smoked a cigarette, finally fell asleep. Seemed like about ten minutes later the deck-hand came and woke me. "Hey, cap," he said. "Midnight."

The most dismal words in the world, the call for night watch. Getting up at midnight is bad enough if you're just a deckhand with no responsibilities, but to stagger up to a strange pilothouse on a strange river—well, no, thanks.

"She's rough and she's tough, Beedle boy, but oh how we love it," Duke said. "Well, call me if you get in trouble." And with this sad farewell he was gone.

My first night watch was a humdinger. I bounced off the bank; I wound up in the trees and backed out. I couldn't see and didn't know what to look for anyway—the mountains towered above me on both sides and cast shadows that looked like islands, and the lights from the coal mines we passed made it even worse. I crawled in and out of a couple of locks, making them the slow old way instead of Duke's flying switch style, and finally, running on a slow bell in an intermittent fog, ran my barge head on into a riverside farmyard and practically into the barn.

I tooted the whistle for a deckhand and National stuck his head in the door, eating a sandwich.

"It's three A.M.," I said, "and I've had enough of this. You get out on the head and I'll hunt up a tree and we'll tie her off."

"Oughta be easy to find a tree, cap," he said. "You found a good many already tonight."

After that I stood a day watch until I found out what this Monongahela looked like, and in a couple of weeks I was running up through fog, smoke, and the black night, smoking cigarettes, hollering for more coffee, and paying no more attention to the river than High Street after midnight back home.

Oh, we had some hair-raisers—it wouldn't be towboating otherwise. One night I was shoving my empty out of Lock 15 and I turned the boat loose and rang a backing bell to get behind the barge so I could face up to shove again. When I rang the come-ahead bell I got no answer and kept right on going back. I rang some more bells but nothing happened and then I opened the door and looked back to see how hard we would hit the lock gates.

The engineer had run out of compressed air to start the Diesel engine and was so mad he was picking Stillson wrenches off the wall and bouncing them off the deck plates. I never heard such a noise or such loud cussing, even in Illinois. That man went clear off his nut he was so mad.

He finally built up some air and we got the engines started again.

After we got hooked up I told National to ask the engineer to come to the pilothouse. He showed up after a while eating a fried egg sandwich.

"You got kind of a hot temper, ain't you?" I said.

"Well, look here," he said. "I see those indicator lights and I hear those bells a-ringin' and I know sure to God I'm all out of air and nothin' to do. Still, you kep' a-ringin' them bells. Cap, that just made me so dang mad I had to do somethin', and I started with the old 8-inch Stillson wrench and I pulled her off the wall and slammed her on the deck. Then I slammed the rest of them and I felt some better."

"Well," I said. "it's a lucky thing there's a film of ice up here above the lock. While you were down there slammin' wrenches on the deck, our barge ran out and stuck in the ice; otherwise she would of gone over the dam."

"How about an egg sandwidge?" he said.

"Okay, thanks," I said. "But don't put no salt on it." And he ducked out into the bitter cold again and fried me up an egg sandwich and we were the best of friends.

A couple of nights later he and the deckhand on watch fell asleep on the galley table, and if I hadn't jumped out of the pilothouse and gone down and yanked them off onto the floor, we would have taken the lock and all right on down to Pittsburgh.

Then we got into high water. Those locks have an open dam beside them, with the water going right over the top like a waterfall.

"There's some bad currents around these here locks in high water, Beedle," Duke told me. "Watch it close when you're comin' down with loads."

I got all messed up at Lock 12 one afternoon and the barge, with 800 tons of coal in it, and the boat commenced drifting crosswise right onto the dam. The cook was making an upsidedown cake and he happened to look out and saw us right on top of the damn and he came hell-bent for the pilothouse and got up on the roof. I pulled the general alarm signal and Duke came up to the pilothouse in his underwear.

I rang the engineer for an overload—for once he wasn't asleep or dreaming—and he really poured it to that old tired-out engine. We hung there with our stern right on the crest of the dam, and finally she began to shove up out of it.

"Well, I ain't gettin' no sleep up here," Duke said, and he went back to bed.

When we got back down to Morgantown that trip, the cook went up the bank and back to home and mother, and then we lived on cheese and crackers for a couple of days until the shore boss sent us a new cook.

This old man was all in from forty-five years in the mines and thought he would make a good steamboat cook. He couldn't cook anything but fried eggs and pork chops, and used the same dishwater for breakfast, lunch, and dinner until it looked like the Chicago drainage canal, so Duke fired him and he went uptown and got a job sweeping out the courthouse on Sundays.

The next cook was out of the mines but he was so dumb they couldn't make a miner out of him, so he came aboard and all he could do was roast. We had roast this and roast that and roast everything but roast eggs. He would throw a chunk of meat and some potatoes and carrots in the roaster and then sit out on the deck all day watching the mountains and the coal mines go past, or reading *Western Detective*.

"Listen, Roast," I said one morning when he was sitting on the floor of the pilothouse carving his fingernails with the paring knife, "why don't you just get down there and make a couple of pies for dinner? Them canned peaches are getting terrible tiresome."

"Cap, if I could cook a pie, what would I be doin' on this here boat? I could easier be boss of the Arkwright mine than I could make a pie." And he went down and stuck a fork in the pork roast and turned over the potatoes.

The Monongahela runs almost straight north to Pittsburgh, where it joins the Allegheny to form the mighty Ohio. We were about a hundred miles from Pittsburgh, at the headwaters up in the mountains, and the river flowed in sharp bends and twists, past coal mines, wild timberland, villages, the B. & O. Railroad yards, and two towns, Morgantown and Fairmont.

We ran into ice and bucked it, and froze in, and broke loose, and finally tied off our load of coal on a smoky Christmas Eve and took the boat down to the Morgantown landing and tied up for Christmas. There was no snow on the ground, and a damp smoky fog hung in the streets as we climbed up the old brick sidewalk to celebrate in a joint called the Imperial.

Seated in a booth and trampled by coal miners with their dome hats on, we drank Kinsey blended whisky with the Tube City beer for chasers, and I thought of home.

That was the worst Christmas I ever put in—everybody had on overalls or $25 blue serge suits, and by midnight they were rolling on the floor and fighting and the girls were drunk and bawling, with their hair coming down, and there were pools of beer and spilled drinks every place. A couple of booths away there was a kid about ten years old who should have been home in bed dreaming of sugar plums—instead he was stealing drinks of beer and was the life of the party.

"How old are you, honey?" I said to my girl Emma, who was smoking cigarettes like her life depended on it.

"How old you think?" she said, draining another shot and chasing it with orange pop.

"Oh, about nineteen," I said, giving her the benefit of the doubt.

"Well, I ain't," she said. "I'm only sixteen. Wahoo! Frank! How's about some service over here?"

So about 2:30, while St. Nick was still busy filling stockings, I went back to my crummy hotel and turned in. Some Christmas Eve.

The winter slowly dragged away, and we had a succession of cooks, and it rained, snowed, sleeted, froze in, thawed, fogged up; and where the sun had gone to nobody seemed to be able to say, but I swear I never saw it for four months at least.

When spring came we opened the bunkroom door a little bit and let some of the fumes escape, tossed some odd shoes in the river, and we were even going to air out the blankets but Duke thought that would fade them. The smoke and fog cleared up for a while, and the sun came out, and I began to get a look at the country, and it was really something to look at. There were trees in bloom in the hills, and mountain laurel with big blossoms on it like I'd never seen before, and the meadows were the greenest green, and the air all through the valley commenced to smell of leaves and flowers instead of soft-coal smoke. With a few trees in leaf around them, these beat-up frame company houses at the mines looked a little better, and the people even seemed less like lost souls; you would see a little girl with a spring hat sitting in the slate piles and it was a big change from winter.

For me to be drawing wages for piloting a towboat under these conditions, why, that's just like paying a kid to watch the circus. The rest of the world was punching the timeclock or shooting holes in each other but here I was all full of roast and Jello, up in a little glass box with nothing to do but steer this cute little boat up and down the river and study the cloud effects over the mountains.

It was kind of a tie which was the most useless, the cook or the second engineer. This engineer I had on my watch was about twenty years old and one of these guys that can't stand to watch you pick your teeth without giving a few pointers.

I was coming downriver one afternoon and he came up to the pilothouse to chew the rag for a while, and we talked about how to make seine nets and whether a horsehair would turn into a snake if you put it in rain water and a raft of other nonsensical topics, and after a while he said, "It ain't none of my business but you ain't in the channel here. You'll find deeper water over yonder."

"That's funny," I said. "Duke told me to run this stretch by holding her right about down the middle."

"It ain't up to me to make no suggestions," he said, "but all the other pilots run close down the left bank until they get down there to the powerhouse."

"All right," I said, and pulled her over toward that deep water he was raving about. In about four minutes the barge began to plow up mud and the engine commenced to labor.

"All of them other pilots must of been dreaming," I said. "In another minute we'll be hard aground."

"Well, I didn't mean quite so far over. Now you got her in too close."

"Okay," I said. "In the meantime would you mind stepping down into the engine room and giving me a backing bell and I'll see if I can work her out of here."

"There used to be plenty of water in here," he said as he left for the engine room.

"I guess it all went for a trip down to Pittsburgh to see a ball game," I said.

And so the spring turned toward summer and it was nearly as hot as Illinois sometimes, and then in midsummer it was all over between me and the Monongahela; they had transferred me again, back to the canal, just in time for the hot weather. I shook hands all around and Duke said, "I'll be seein' you over there, kid. I ain't gonna stay here in these West Virginia wilderness forever," and I packed up my old suitcase and got on the two-car steam train for Connellsville, Pa., where the express for Chicago came through.

The train followed right along the riverbank, and pretty soon I saw the boat coming up from Rosedale with a load, with that old stack kind of pushed back and a cloud of blue exhaust trailing behind, and as we passed abreast of her I saw Duke up in the glass box, and National out coiling down a line on the barge, and Roast was lying down on the deck sound asleep. I wanted to holler at Duke and say, "So long, Duke, meet me up at the Imperial," and "So long, Roast, don't forget them canned peaches," and I wanted to tell the guy sitting beside me here in the train, "That's Duke Harmison up in the pilothouse, he's the captain. And that's the cook asleep there. He's a no-good bum. They must have about eight hundred tons in that barge—looks like Rosedale coal. That deckhand's name is Clarence Adams but we call him National. And I'm the pilot."

Then in a second we had passed them, and they faded in the distance, and that was the end of me and the tow-boat *Coal Queen* and the Monongahela River, Duke Harmison, and the coal mines.

"See that old boat?" said the fellow in overalls beside me on the green plush. "Ain't it a miracle what some fools will do to earn a living? Can you imagine living on a thing like that?"

"Yeh," I said, "I can imagine it."

Chapter 2

It's Rough Going Back

But that wasn't the end of the Monongahela River and me because once you have lived on a river and steamboated on it, seen the fog hanging by the shore at dawn and heard the clear ice cracking in the wintertime, that river is part of you and you never lose it. You can steamboat clear to Fort Benton on the Missouri or up the Yukon from Alakanuk to Whitehorse, but you still think of the other rivers and you want to go back but you can't. Because you know you're not going back for keeps and to go back for a visit is no good.

So now I hear they've put in a new dam at Morgantown. Well, they can't change it like they changed Duck River Suck when they put in Kentucky Dam down on the Tennessee but it won't be the same and you'd have to start all over. Duke and Roast are gone off to carve out their destinies in some other far-off valley and the *Coal Queen* has gone back to the Illinois River and lies sunk with the fish playing hide-and-seek in the engine room.

Mark Twain went back years after he was a pilot and

took a ride on the Upper Mississippi and had to pad out
with anecdotes he picked up from the pilots and the stew-
ard. Of course he was Lower Mississippi to his toes. So he
went back to the Lower Mississippi and took a ride and he
found everything different, pilot friends dead, cutoffs and
crossings all changed, and to a riverman it is sad stuff and
makes him feel old.

You don't get to know a river by riding along its banks
in a car and taking snapshots, or by going down it in a
canoe with a patent cookstove, or even by reading books
about it, like this one although all these things are a help.
And the least productive way of knowing a river is to get
aboard a 50-foot cabin cruiser and spend a weekend among
the ice cubes and ash trays with a bunch of friends in loud
sport shirts who want to play canasta all the time.

In order to have a river in your blood, unforgettably
and forever, like a love for the track or a feeling for pit
bulls, you have to work on her for wages. You have to sweat
it out in the dirty night when any sane person would be
home in the parlor reading the papers. You have to rise up
at dawn and smell the night smells turning to day smells.
You have to hear the engineers hollering at each other
down in the engine room and listen to your whistle echo-
ing off the hills in the early spring evenings. You've got to
eat it, sleep it, hate it, and breathe it until you've got river
in your shoe soles and in your pants pockets.

Sure, I've been back to the Monongahela.

It took a lot of hunting but I finally found one of the
boys. He was coming down the muddy street with one

of those miner's caps on and I was sitting on the steps of a company house waiting for him.

"Hi, National," I said. "I thought you wasn't never going into them coal mines."

"Well, for the— Don't tell me you're back here on them steamboats again. How are you, Mr. Pilot!"

"I'll make it," I said.

"You're gettin' fat."

"Aren't we all."

"Where you at now?"

"Over on the Upper Mississippi. A thousand miles away."

"Come on. Let's go have some beer." He dumped his lunch bucket on the porch.

The old lady came out on the porch.

"Come on," he said.

"You goin' off and get drunk again now I expect," says the old lady.

"That's right," he said.

We walked down the middle of the street between the frame houses.

"Where's Gas?" I said.

"Oh, him. He went up to Uniontown. He's drivin' a truck last I heard."

"What about Roast?"

"Why, didn't you hear? He fell asleep layin' out there on deck like he use to do, rolled into the river by mistake and drownded. Up by Lock 15."

"The hell he did."

"Yes, he did. He sure did. Dead as a hunk of slate."

"How about that hot-tempered engineer? What's his name?"

"Jeff Wilson? Oh, he wandered over the mountains someplace. I ain't seen him in two years. I expect he's makin' somebody's life miserable with advice."

"Well, they're all gone. And you're in the mines."

"Yeah, they're all gone. But where's Duke?"

"He's still at it. He's running sand and gravel, they say, down on the Ohio someplace."

"Them was the days wasn't they, Beedle? She was some old river."

"She was that, kid."

"But where you at now, what you doin'?"

"Well, after I left here I did a little more steamboatin' out on the Illinois. Then I come back here to the hills and went to firing a locomotive on the Western Maryland but I got a cinder in my eye and quit. After that I took a run around the Great Lakes on one of them ore freighters as a deckhand. Then I went to work in a factory in Cleveland and, boy, in a factory after being out in the fresh air all your life, why, that's like being sent to the Siberian salt mines."

"Where is them mines? What union they got?"

"Never mind, it's no good anyway."

"What you doin' over here?"

"Well, I'm writin' a book, believe it or not."

"I ain't surprised none. Next year I imagine you'll be walkin' the high wire with Cole Brothers Circus. What you writin' a book about, Beedle?"

"About the Monongahela River."

"What? Why, man, how can you write a whole book just about that dang ole river?"

"That's the question, kid, how can I write a whole book just about the Monongahela?"

"How come you writin' a book?"

"Well, I'll tell you, while I was in that factory I got so homesick for a breath of fresh air and the sound of a steamboat whistle and a deckhand snoring that I sat down and wrote up a little story on our adventures on the *Coal Queen*."

"Adventures is right. So you sold it, hey?"

"Yeah man, I sold her."

"How much did they give you?"

"They give me two hundred."

"Wahoo! Let's go over to the company store and get a pencil and a tablet. I b'lieve I'll set down and write me a story too."

"You couldn't do it, National. You'd pretty it up too much."

"No, I reckon I couldn't."

Then we didn't say much for a while. The joint was all jampacked with miners and miners' wives and miners' girl friends and miners' kids, and outside, beyond the muddy street where they had thrown down a few cinders, down at the end of the street was the Monongahela. It was another dirty gray afternoon; just such a one as that time, now so long ago it seemed, when I had come down to the bank and had my first look at the *Coal Queen*. But you can't bring those things back—it's always too late. Life drags you along by the collar and no use to look behind.

"I see the Mon is still down there runnin' past town," I said.

"Yeah," he said. "But the *Coal Queen* is gone. It don't seem the same no more somehow."

So you see it's rough going back. But sometime or other you have to do it.

The first thing I did after being elected to write this book was go see my great-uncle Bud, who is the last of the Chippewa River pilots and a historian to boot. The last trip he made down the Chippewa was in the fall of 1893 on a barn door with a 16-foot pike pole for power. "The water was so low I even had to portage that dang door twice," he told me.

"Well," says Bud, "if you're going to write a book just get a card in the Public Library and say good-bye to the wife and kids. You're going to be so bothered and so mean from now on you better not plan on going home at all. I'll tell you what I'll do," says Bud. "I'll give you the upper bunk on the *Eau Claire Belle* and you can live with me until you are done with all the heavy brain work."

The *Eau Claire Belle* is the shanty boat he lives on. It was built at St. Cloud up the Minnesota River about six years before Paul Bunyan took his first swipe at a white pine tree and has been rebuilt as many times as the *Constitution*.

"Are you still tied up in front of the brewery, Bud?" I said.

"Yes," he said, "and in the evenings I will entertain

you with humorous and tragic stories of the old raft days."

But I turned Bud down and holed up in the Public Library and am all ready now to bust loose with the true facts on the beautiful Monongahela including the Indians and their gory habits, and poor old Braddock, and General Forbes, and the first long-stroking steamboats, and the tide of crazy humans that stampeded down through the valley, and rye whisky, and Mr. Carnegie's battle with Mr. Frick, and the coal mines, and Captain Shreve, and the Combine and her Big Spills, and Low Water, and Mrs. Nicholas Roosevelt's baby, and the engineer's bathrobe, and the *Sprague* and the *Boaz* and the *Alice Brown* and all the other lovely steamboats, the big blowup at Monongah, and all the rest of it.

It's exciting and awful and dirty and beautiful up the Monongahela. In the evenings you can see the lights of the miners' houses strung up and down the hills, the sky reddens with a hellish glow from the steel mills, and a steamboat blows for the lock and the lonesome note echoes up and down the valley and makes you feel very funny, about half sad and half thrilled.

A miner stands on the back porch in his suspenders looking down the street. A train puffs up the valley dragging a string of empty coal cars. IRON CITY BEER says a red sign in the sky. Carnegie, Jones & Laughlin, American Steel & Wire, Weirton Steel! Coal and more coal. Steel! Billets, blooms, sheet bars and skelp, forging steel, junior beams, pipe, casing, bars, spikes, tie plates, angles, channels, tees, zees, spring wire, rods, annealed wire, coke tin plate, screw stock, and shafting.

And coal. Thirty million tons of it moving down the Monongahela every year. Thirty million tons. Not counting what's moved in those long trains that drag up and down the valley with thunderous snorts night and day. That's a lot of coal.

Oh, it's some wonderful valley, the Monongahela. There's more hell popping and more loud noise in any ten miles at the lower end than there is in five hundred on the Mississippi or the Congo.

You go into a saloon and they're talking six different languages and the juke box is blasting out a tune in Slovenian by Yankoviç. Across the street are the torn green shades of a faded brick building and the third-generation Polish girls tripping lightly along the sidewalk in their blue jeans and costume jewelry. Ragged hillsides with the bare frame houses clinging to the rocky slope, where you dump the dishwater off the back porch and it lands on the roof of the house below. Winter nights so cold the train whistles freeze up, and lovers seek shelter in the motion-picture palaces. And always the miners and the steelworkers—raw, rough, and roaring out their protests and their manhood against the smoke and flames.

And the chimneys of the zinc mills, the glassworks, the chemical plants, the rolling mills and wire and tube and steel mills and coke plants are snorting their poisonous mixtures into the scarred and terrifying hills. Twenty people died in the smog up at Donora in '48 in the greasy fumes—six thousand lay abed gasping. The train whistles blow and the Carnegie-Illinois steamboats and the Jones & Laughlin steamboats blow their lock whistles and landing whistles, and the interurbans blast their horns and the trucks moving coal and oil and glass and beer add to the uproar—oh, it's gay up the Mon, mighty gay.

Chapter 3

Inhabitants of the Great Forest

The most prominent feature of the trans-Allegheny frontier when the first white men pushed into the area, was the vast and seemingly endless virgin forest, which extended from the mountains westward in an unbroken mass as far west as Lexington, Ky., in the south and Indianapolis in the north. This enormous tract of timber is referred to by historians as "The Great Forest" or the "Black Forest of America."

It was part of what modern foresters call the "Central Forest," and it was a hardwood forest, which contained more different kinds of trees than any other in North America. There were a few stands of isolated softwood or evergreen trees—shortleaf pine is the most important to-day—and there are also pitch pines and red cedar,—but the distinguishing characteristic of this forest was that it was a hardwood forest. All the other forests of North America save this one are either entirely softwoods or predominantly softwoods with a light mixture of hardwoods. Oaks were the most abundant in the Great Forest, and grew to enormous size. Other valuable trees which composed

FIGURE 2. THE MONONGAHELA JUST ABOVE PITTSBURGH DISTRICT, 1943.

this rich timberland were hickory, yellow poplar, walnut, ash, elm, and of lesser commercial value there were several hundred other species. Today less than five per cent of the original forest remains.

Francis Parkman says of the Great Forest that "one vast continuous forest shadowed the fertile soil, covering the land as the grass covers the garden lawn, sweeping over hill and hollow in endless undulation, burying mountains in verdure, and mantling brooks and rivers from the light of day." Professor Archer Butler Hulbert also makes an interesting comment on the character of this wilderness: "The most impressive characteristic of the old forest was the absence of undergrowth; this could not live without sunlight, and the sunlight could not pierce through the dense overgrowth. This density of treetops was, also, an impressive feature of the old forest, since almost every tree was loaded with vines, especially those of the grape; these vines revelled in the sunshine found at the treetops and ran riot from one tree to another. The Black Forest has most frequently been characterized as a 'pathless wilderness' and a 'howling wilderness'; it is difficult to tell what a 'howling wilderness' might be unless it be a wilderness infested with beasts that howl; wolves howled in the old Ohio Valley but the forests as a rule were marvellously silent—a silence intensified tenfold when now and then the howl of a hungry wolf broke its deathly reign."

But long before the Great Forest had spread over the land there was another forest, a forest composed of Lepidodendron, Sigillaria, Cordaites, Calamites and other curious trees and giant ferns that no man has ever seen, because they grew some millions of years ago. In geologic time this is the Pennsylvanian Period, during which the coal measures of North America were deposited, probably by biochemical decomposition of the ancient forests under swamp conditions, followed by dynamochemical processes such as heat and pressure. By such means were the fabulous coal seams of the Monongahela region formed.

Much later, in the Tertiary Period, the erosion of the Cretaceous peneplain of the east began, and has continued ever since, dissecting this upland belt and forming the Appalachian Mountains. At the same time archaic mammals were roaming the forests and grassy plains—such curious creatures as creodonts, glyptodonts, and condylarths. Followed the ice age and some thousands of years of tedious progress until Homo sapiens came to the Monongahela.

But we will forge ahead, not stopping to trace the legends of the prehistoric North American aborigines, and listen to one of the very first reports by a white man, on the Monongahela River itself—Lewis Evans speaking, in 1750:

> Ohio has many branches, which furnish good navigation to the adjacent parts, but the most considerable of these is the Monaungahela much distinguished by its Royley Water which joins the Ohio (or Allegeni) near the confines of this Province. The land between the Forks of the Ohio is low swampy ground, much infested with venomous Serpents and Muskeetose, and subject to be overflowed every spring; but the land surrounding is very high (I had almost said mountainous) so that a noble prospect

may be had from any point. The River Youghiogani joins the Monaungahela at some distance above the Forks and as it descends from the direction of the Potowmack is likely in time to become a link in the sole passage from Ohio to the Ocean.

This is probably not the earliest description of the Monongahela, but it will suffice. "Royley" means roiled up and hence muddy. This is at some variance with the Monongahela school of poetic writers of later years who were fond of submitting poems in the genteel and romantic style to the local papers in the nineteenth century and who usually got in some heavy work in the "Oh, limpid Monongahela!" and "Ah, blue Monongahela!" vein. As to the present complexion of the river, in the upper end it is pretty clear most of the time; I mean it is pretty clear for a river, and whereas it does not sparkle like a stream out in the Grand Tetons, still it does not resemble a mud road in liquid suspension like the Lower Mississippi. At the lower end, what with one thing and another being dumped in it, it is probably as powerful a brew as the one the witches cooked up in *Macbeth*. If this is not so, I apologize in advance to the Pittsburgh Department of Health and Sanitation. I understand however, that the last fish made his getaway from the Monongahela about one hundred years ago.

The inhabitants of this country in 1750 were a mixed group, living a life of brutish discomfort. They consisted of scattered groups of wild Indians (whose numbers were already being reduced by "Starvation, Rum, and fowl Diseases carried in by the traders"), equally wild Indian traders ("the most vicious and abandoned Wretches of our Nation and the Indians hold them in great contempt as a Set of Mean Dishonest mercenary Fellows"), occasional stray French and English explorers and military chaps, and considerable quantities of wild cats, wolves, deer, and other woodland dwellers (although the "skin Trade" had already wiped out so many deer that "nearly every Winter hath become a Starving Time for the Indian Nations"), as well as an abundant and very healthy population of venomous reptiles and "stinging flies and divers other Insects." These shuffled to and fro in the trackless wilderness attempting to avoid each other's company as much as possible, and most of them hungry and miserable a good part of the time. The white men stood in immediate peril night and day of losing the tops of their heads to the scalping knife, the Indians faced daily prospect of instant destruction from various conflicts, the animals' life expectancy was negligible, and the only truly contented creatures seem to have been the "Muskeetose."

Even after 1770, long after the argument with the French had been ended and the difference of opinion with Pontiac settled, things were still rough and rugged out in this country. Here are some recollections of a man whose parents moved into the Upper Monongahela territory, up around Morgantown, in 1773:

"The next I recollect our family was living in the Monongahela Glades near Decker's Creek. As soon as war broke we had to leave the place and the whole family went to Kearn's Fort opposite where Morgantown now stands. My father then had eight negroes. We planted and raised corn on the ground where Morgantown now stands.

"This was a stockaded fort. While living there Coburn Fort, about two miles this side of Kearn's Fort, was burnt by the Indians. I was at it when on fire. How it happened I was suffered to go I cannot tell.

"Miller and Woodfin were killed on Miller's place, three miles from Kearn's Fort while we were there. They were brought into the fort on poles, having their feet and hands tied and the pole running between them.

"While living at Kearn's Fort, we had small pox in the natural way—all the family except my father who had had it. Two children, I think, were all that died then with that disease.

"While living in this fort, we boys would go out on what we called the Hogback near the fort to hunt ramps. We used the bow and arrow and were very good in shooting them.

"Once while standing in the yard some one shot up an arrow straight; it fell and struck through the wrist of either Colonel John Evans or one of the Wilsons; it was hard to get out. This is all the accidents I recollect happening while we lived at the fort.

"During what was called the hard winter, the snow was very deep, we lived in a large old house on Johnson's land—it had two doors. I remember we would draw logs in the house with our horse 'Prince' and roll them back on the fire. We had a number of deer skins hung around the house to keep the wind off.

"In those days we wore short breeches and leggings,

what else I do not recollect. How we lived I have only an indistinct recollection. I remember once when brother John and myself went to Ruble's Mills in Pennsylvania. Some one there gave us each a piece of light bread with butter. This I thought such a great feast that I have it in my mind to this day.

"While we were living on Joseph's land, David Morgan killed the two Indians. They sent my father a piece of tanned Indian skin for a strap. I was with my father at the rope works making cords to make a hoppose.

"Thomas Laidley and McNeely had brought a store to Morgantown. My father bought a bear-skin coat, as he had to go to Williamsburgh to be examined.* The morning before he started, Laidley, and Menes, his storekeeper, came to our house with, I believe 20 half-joes, in all $200 in gold, to send to Richmond to buy land warrants. I remember hearing my father say he was afraid to wear said coat for fear people would think he was proud."

None of this is very funny: Indians, smallpox in the natural way, Miller and Woodfin carried home on poles, tanned Indian skin—the outlook is one of grim and unfunny realities.

In a compendium of contemporary letters, journals, and other firsthand documents (the Draper Manuscript Collection of the Wisconsin Historical Society), we find a continuing catalogue of disasters on the trans-Allegheny frontier. This in 1777:

"Aug. 2. Charles Grigsby's wife & child were killed and scalped.

* For service in the Revolutionary War.

"Aug. 11. One settler was killed and scalped last Friday near Blackmore's on the Clinch River.

"Aug. 13. On stepping to the door, John Carnahan was instantly shot dead.

"Seeing an Indian pursuing him, Caldwell wrenched himself loose with great effort, just as the Indian threw his tomahawk, which missed its aim, and Caldwell escaped to Shepherds Fort six miles up the creek.

"John Boyd, a youth, was killed with their tomahawks and scalped.

"Young Shepherd [only nineteen], as he neared the fort, his foot caught in a grapevine, and before he could recover, the Indians tomahawked and scalped him.

"On the 13th Instant at Coone's Fort on the West Fork the Indians killed and scalped a woman only 150 yards from the Fort, and appeared to be Very Impudent.

"The Wiondots and Mingos are all gone home again according to their Knowledge they killed 14 People at Weelunk.

"They have killed two men, one child, & one negro, & have taken a little girl prisoner from Greenbriar.

"In 1779 Indians murdered his daughters Fanny and Phebe as they were taking dinner to men in the hayfield."

All of these unhappy events (and I have only scratched the surface) took place in the vicinity of Pittsburgh during and just after the Revolutionary War. One can scarcely find more lugubrious reading anywhere in history, than in some of these detailed reports of murder on the new frontier of the Upper Ohio.

What in tarnation were these folks doing here in the first place? Better to be poor, even crushed by society in Philadelphia, I should think, than to live in a precinct where you can't step out of the house without getting your hair parted with an ax. But as one authority says: "Nearly everyone there drank heavily, and almost everyone was a fugitive, if not from justice, certainly from creditors. Drunken Indians staggered through the village . . . and white traders were unabashed with temporary wives, some of them squaws."

However, in addition to the "reprobate traders" and other such specimens, there were a few frontiersmen of the James Fenimore Cooper pattern, such as John Frazer, whose original place was on French Creek up Allegheny River way at Venango, and who subsequently removed, by request, to the Monongahela; William Trent and George Croghan ("This last is a Dublin Irishman who is a mere Idol among his countrymen, the Irish traders, and the Indians from whom he has taken a Squaw to wife, and is said to controul one-fourth the Trade of the Ohio Country and to have many servants and factors and associates and to have hundreds of Pack-horses for the hawling of his Trade-goods"); as well as the famous Christopher Gist.

Gist was a very paragon of a frontiersman right out of the works of Harry Castlemon. He could apparently lick his weight in lions, perforate a squirrel at a quarter of a mile range, and construct a woodland shelter at a moment's notice. More impressive is the fact that he could read and write, and even kept a journal of his activities.

Here is what Douglas Southall Freeman has to say about Gist in his exhaustive and thoroughly entertaining biography of George Washington:

"His character became his varied roles. Adversity never seemed to depress him. If he had to write in his journal of sickness or of delay on account of weather, he always added an optimistic antithesis: He was sick, but he recovered; he had been kept in camp by rain, but he had killed a bear. Although not healthy, he had vast endurance. Solitary as his daily life was, he had been known to leave an Indian town and to sleep in the forest, rather than keep the company of those he denounced as 'reprobate traders.' No frontiersman understood the Indians better or had greater patience in dealing with them. Gist was a good shot, a fine hunter who seldom went hungry if there was any game in the woods, and he had a quick eye for good land. Few could excel him in making himself comfortable in the wilderness, as, for example, when he drove a panther from its lair under an overhanging rock and slept cheerfully there a January night in 1752.

"Gist was a man of some education and of religious principles, reared in the Church of England; but he was accustomed to view stoically the ways of savages he knew he could not reform. In the Wyandot town at the Muskingum, Christmas Day, 1750, Gist held what probably was the first Protestant religious service in the region destined to become the State of Ohio. The next day he had to stand passively by while the natives loosed a captive Indian woman whose fate he thus described: ' . . . The persons appointed for the purpose pursued her and struck her on the ear, on the right side of her head, which beat her flat on her face on the ground; they then stuck her several times through the back to the heart, scalped her, and threw the scalp in the air, and another cut off her head.' The Indians who were capable of this were devoted to Gist, whom they named Annosanah. This, they said, 'was a name of a good man that had formerly lived among them.'

"Washington was to find Gist capable of handling both compass and canoe, a man altogether conscientious in the performance of duty and, at the same time, not disposed to volunteer counsel on matters entrusted to his young companion. He would advise George when asked; otherwise he would leave the young Adjutant to make decisions unless the circumstances involved an element of danger with which Washington was unacquainted. More than any other man, Gist was to be George's teacher in the art of the frontiersman who had to deal with the uncertain savages. George scarcely could have had a better instructor: he had now to demonstrate how apt a pupil he would be."

Apropos of the frontier, I want to close this chapter with an excerpt from a letter written by Samuel Allen, who crossed the Alleghenies by Braddock's old road with his wife and child in search of good luck and fortune in the year of 1796. Here it is:

"Belleville, Virginia, November
the 15th, 1796
"Honored Parents:
". . . When we arrived to Allexandria [Alexandria,

Virginia] Mr. Avory found that taking land cariag from there to the Monongehaly would be less expence than it would be to go any farther up the Potomac and less danger so he hired wagoners to carry the goods across the mountains to Mogantown on the Mongahaly about one hundred miles above Pittsburg. Mr. Avorys expence in comeing was from N. London to Alexandria six dollars each for the passengers and two shillings & six pence for each hundred weight. from Alexandria to Morgantown was thirty two shillings and six pence for each hundred weight of women and goods the men all walked the hole of the way. I walked the hole distance it being almost three hundred miles and we found the road to be pritty good untill we came to the mountaing. crossing the blue Mountain the Monongehaly & the Lorral Mountains we found the roads to be verry bad.

"You doubtless remember I rote in my last letter that Prentice was taken ill a day or two before he continued verry much so untill the 10th of July when he began to gro wors the waggoner was hired by the hundred weight and could not stop unless I paid him for the time that he stoped & for the Keeping of the horses that I could not afford to do so we were obliged to keep on. We were now on the Allegany Mountain & a most horrid rode the wagon golted so that I dare not let him ride So I took him in my arms and carried him all the while except once in a while Mr. Davis would take him in his armes & carry him a spell to rest me. a young man that Mr. Avory hired at Allexandria a joiner whose kindness I shall not forgit he kep all the while with us & spared no panes to assist us in anything

& often he offer himself, our child at this time was verry
sick & no medical assistance could be had on this mountain
on the morning of the 13th as we was at breackfast at the
house of one Mr. Tublestone the child was taken in a fit
our company had gone to the next house to take breakfast
which was one mile on our way we were alone in the room
& went & asked Mrs. Tumblestone to come into the room
she said she did not love to see a person in a fitt . . . Mr.
Tumblestone spoke in a verry lite manner & sayes with a
smile it will save you the trouble of carrying it any farther
if it does die. We then bundled up the child and walked to
the next house ware we come up with our company . . .
The man of the house gave it some drops that stopped the
fitt. He handed me a vial of the dropps—gave directions
how to use them the child had no more fitts but seemed to
be stupid.

"When we took dinner it was six mile to the next
house the waggoners said they could not get thro that
night we did not love to stay out for fear our child would
die in the woods so we set off & left the waggons. I took the
child in my arms and we traveled on Mr. Davis set off with
us and carried the child above half the time here we traveled up & down the most edious [hideous?] hills as I ever
saw & by nine oclock in the evening we came to the house
the child continued stayed all night the next morning at
break of day I perceived it grew worse in two hours the
child dyed Polly was obliged to go rite off as soon as his
eyes was closed for the waggoners would not stop I stayed
to see the child buried I then went on two of the men that
was with me were joiners & had their tools with them they

stayed with me & made the coffin Mr. Simkins the man of the house sent his Negroes out & dug the grave whare he had burried several strangers that dyed a crossing the mountain he family all followed the corps to the grave black & white & appeared much affected.

"When we returned to the house I asked Mr. Simkins to give me the name and the name of the place he asked me the name of the child I told him he took his pen & ink & rote the following lines Aligany County Merriland July the 14th 1796 died John P. Allen at the house of John Simkins at atherwayes bear complain broadaggs [Braddock's] old road half way between fort Cumberland & Uniontown.

"We left the city of Alexandria on the Potomac the 30th day of June & arrived at Morgantown on the Monongahely the 18th day of July.

"When we arrived at Morgantown the river was so low that boats could not go down but it began to rain the same day that I got there I was about one mile from there when it began to rain & from the 22nd at night to the 23rd in the morning it raised 16 feet the logs came down the river so that it was dangerous for boats to go & on Sunday the 22nd in the evening the boats set off three waggons had not arrived but the river was loreing so fast that we dare not wate the goods was left with a Merchant in that town to be sent when the river rises they have not come on yet one of my barrels & the brass Cittle is yet behind."

Chapter 4

Flatboats, Keelboats, and Other Strange Creatures

By the latter half of the eighteenth century the English colonies in America had a population of over a million. The French population was only sixty-five thousand but in spite of the inequality in numbers the French caused a great deal of trouble. In order to prevent English occupation of the Upper Ohio Valley the French built a fort on the point between the Allegheny and Monongahela where Pittsburgh now stands; they called it Fort Duquesne and indicated their intention to remain.

Across from England to dislodge the French came General Edward Braddock, a rather crusty English military man with a low opinion of everything American, especially Indians and frontiersmen, whom he considered "crudely dressed, ill-mannered, and undisciplined." When Benjamin Franklin advised Braddock to beware of Indian ambuscades, Braddock replied with a smile, "These savages may, indeed, be a formidable enemy to your raw American militia, but upon the King's regular and disciplin'd troops, sir, it is impossible they should make any impression."

After dragging with ghastly effort four 12-pound cannon, six six-pounders, four howitzers, and fifteen cohorn mortars over the wild Alleghenies, Braddock's king's regulars were ambushed only nine miles from Fort Duquesne, on July 9, 1754, by a force of ill-mannered French and Indian woods fighters who poured lead into the redcoats in parade-ground formation, at such a rate that sixty-three of the eighty-five officers were killed or wounded. Five hundred regulars were lost, the rest fled back down the road and across the Monongahela. Braddock, rescued by his aides after five horses had been shot from under him and he had received a mortal wound, said, "We shall better know how to deal with them another time." In twenty minutes he was dead, the classic example of military disaster in the American woods.

Four years later, in 1758, General John Forbes led another expedition on Fort Duquesne, this time through the mud and rough terrain of western Pennsylvania. He took an unusually large army and when reports came in via scouts to the French fort, the commander decided the time had come to evacuate. Without firing a shot Forbes advanced to the strategic point of land on which the eyes of Europe had been so long fixed, and occupied it in the name of the crown. The next day he named the place Fort Pitt and the reconstruction of the ruined fort was begun.

From this time, 1758, through the Revolutionary War, and until the beginning of the nineteenth century, things were extremely lively out in this area in the matter of Indians, murders, and other exciting competitions as described in the preceding chapter. In 1764 Governor John

Penn declared open season the year round on Indians and gave impetus to the sport by offering bounties as follows:

Males above ten years captured	$150
Scalps of ditto	134
Females, and males under the ten-year age limit captured	130
Scalps of females	50

And yet more and more emigrants pushed westward across the mountains to Redstone or Pittsburgh, willing to take their chances against the perils of the wilderness.

In 1787 the Congress of the Confederation passed the Northwest Ordinance, throwing open to settlement the lovely rich territory now composing the states of Ohio, Illinois, Indiana, Michigan, and Wisconsin. Although they knew little or nothing of conditions in the west, hundreds of thousands of dwellers in the original seacoast colonies packed up the iron kettle and candlesticks and decided to go out west and remove a few forests, grow some corn eighteen feet tall, start up a few states, build a few dozen railroads, have a look at that there Ohio River, and maybe send a buffalo hide home. Of course the wives objected to leaving Bridgeport or Trenton or Baltimore "just when we're getting the house paid for at last," but when the men promised to become governors of the new states and to make oversize fortunes the ladies decided to come along.

The easiest way to get out to the new hunting grounds was over the mountains, either over the National Road to Brownsville or over Forbes' Road to Pittsburgh, and thence down the Ohio, which flowed beside the shores of the territory for nearly a thousand miles, and by means of many of whose tributaries one could penetrate directly into the heart of the country for some considerable distances.

Arrived at Pittsburgh or Brownsville, they found the major problem was only to build or buy a boat, pile wife, kids, mattresses, dogs, hogs, old brindle cow, plow, grindstone, kettles, 25 pounds of bacon, and a keg of Old Monongahely aboard, turn loose, and drift down to the Promised Land. In the early period the travelers often felled trees and built their boats themselves, which must have resulted in some queer rigs and probably unexpected sinkings en route. But almost immediately boatbuilders, ship's carpenters, calkers and other marine craftsmen from the estuaries, bays, and sounds of the eastern shores set up shop on the Monongahela and began to turn out water transportation at a great rate. And as the stampede westward continued, there were built at Monongahela and Allegheny River shipyards, and at shipyards on the Upper Ohio, literally tens of thousands of various styles of flatboats and keelboats. The Monongahela yards, particularly at Elizabeth, Brownsville, and Pittsburgh, were in business on a scale exceeding all others in providing boats for the seemingly endless hordes of pilgrims.

The boats built were of various types but the cheapest were flatboats and these were the standard family conveyance, although other boats were built such as pirogues, skiffs, bateaux, keelboats, arks, broadhorns, barges, packet boats, Kentucky boats, New Orleans boats, and mixed varieties combining selected features of the above, but all having one chief and painful characteristic of being nonself-propelled. Almost all of these ungainly water bugs were one-way trippers: they were built, floated downstream on the bosom of the Belle Rivière and the not-so-belle Mississippi, reached the end of the line and were broken up for their timber. The only boats which moved in both directions on the rivers were the keelboats, which were pushed upstream by human beings (part human anyway) shoving on setting poles, and sometimes aided by a favorable wind in their crude sails.

The hazards of navigation to these intrepid voyagers from farms and mills and shops of the east were many, and of assorted colors, sizes, and prices. Getting over the mountains was no simple task in itself, especially with small children, babies, bewildered and apprehensive lady folks, and perhaps a crotchety grandfather or great-aunt ever ready with a shilling's worth of advice; and the travelers arrived along the Monongahela sometimes exhausted and out of sorts. If the weather were fine, they had here a chance to recuperate, wash up and rest; but if the weather were cold, the hardships of the emigrants, lined up for miles on the roads approaching the ice-covered Monongahela, were painful indeed.

If the head of the family had a dollar to spare before embarking he would buy a copy of Zadok Cramer's "The NAVIGATOR, Containing Directions for Navigating THE MONONGAHELA, ALLEGHENY, OHIO, and MISSISSIPPI RIVERS, with an AMPLE ACCOUNT OF THESE MUCH ADMIRED WATERS, from the head of the former to the mouth of the latter; and a concise description of their *Towns, Villages, Harbors, Settlements,*

&c. with Maps of the Ohio and Mississippi." This famous book was available at Cramer's bookstore on Market Place in Pittsburgh and at other jumping-off places, and ran into many editions, for years and years, as long as the traffic westward continued to pour down the Ohio Valley.

Some of the "directions for navigating" are a little bit alarming, and if read to while away the time and improve the mind while waiting for the take-off, must have surely awakened some apprehension in the more timid. "The first thing to be attended to by emigrants . . . is to procure a boat, to be ready so as to take advantage of the times of flood, and to be careful that the boat be a good one: For many of the accidents that happen in navigating the Ohio, are owing to the unpardonable carelessness or penuriousness of the boat-builders, who frequently slight their work, or make their boats of injured plank; in either case putting the lives and properties of a great many people at manifest hazard."

This is a nice paragraph to turn over in the mind in the middle of the night somewhere below Wheeling while listening to the ominous gurgling of the current against the hull.

In case of running ice in the river "it is safest to permit your boat to have pretty much her own way, as rowing may tend to throw you out of the current or on points of islands, before you are aware of it; in which case nothing but presence of mind and great exertions will save you." In other words, if you get caught in an ice jam, just let the ice knock your boat (with all your loved ones and earthly possessions aboard) about and slam it and turn it around while you wonder again if the penurious boatbuilder has included some "injured plank" in your ark, and if so just how soon the ice is going to get to it.

However, in case you decide to work your way out of the ice and tie up for the night it is advised that you find a small point and tie up below it. "By bringing to in such a situation, and fixing your canoe (or skiff) above the boat, with one end strongly tied down to the shore, and the other out in the stream, sloping downwards, so as to drive off the cakes of ice, which would otherwise accumulate, and tend to sink or drive your boat from her moorings, you may lie with a tolerable degree of safety.

"This is a much better way than of felling a tree above the boat so as to partly fall in the river; for if the tree does not strongly adhere to the stump, ten to one but the masses of ice carry it down against your boat, and put you in imminent danger, much worse than if the precaution had not been taken." And ten to one but the captain would be in imminent danger of receiving the cast-iron frying pan over the head from friend wife.

In regard to trimming the boat, cheerful old Zadok says: "Though the construction of our boats does not render them liable to overset, yet when loaded irregularly, and one corner sunken more than another, a stroke on a rock, or a log on the diagonal corner, subjects her to fill in that quarter much sooner than if properly trimmed."

After several more pages of lugubrious alarms, Zadok ends his dissertation on the pleasures of river travel with a dime's worth of morality: "For the greater part of the accidents that happen on the Ohio, arise from a want of proper knowledge of the means that ought to be taken to prevent them. Some, indeed, possessing the knowledge, unpardonably neglect their duty, until sad experience puts them in mind of it, by a loss which they are little able to bear."

It has been estimated that about fifteen hundred emigrants were murdered by Indians while en route down the river in flatboats. To avoid losing their lives many took to forming "brigades" or fleets of boats lashed together. Denny's *Military Journal* of 1790 tells of a flotilla of sixteen "Kentucky boats" and two keelboats which were made up with the flats three abreast, and the keels on either flank for protection. The women and children were stowed in the boats in the middle of the fleet, while the men stood watch in the keels and outside flats. Working a conglomeration of this kind down the river must have required a lot of sweat on the sweeps, unless they came down on a fresh, when the main problem must have been getting her stopped.

This big emigration had started before the Revolution, was interrupted by it, but resumed afterwards in greatly increased numbers. As the Monongahela was the main highway, many prosperous boatyards were established on its banks. These yards continued to flourish until late in the nineteenth century. During the forties and fifties it is probable that there was not a navigable stream on the western waterway system which did not feel the cutwater of a Monongahela-built craft.

Besides the one-way downstream westward traffic, there was considerable upstream service offered by the man-propelled keelboat, both during the pre-steamboat era and for many years after the arrival of steam. The keelboat was the only craft built with any "lines," symmetry, or marine elegance, and was long and of comparatively narrow beam; most of the other craft on the western rivers looked like piano boxes, floating sheds, or errant lumber piles. The keelboat had a cabin for passengers and was propelled by men shoving on "setting poles."

On the Monongahela proper the keelboat completely dominated the local trade and maintained a very lucrative business long after the soot-throwing paddle-wheelers invaded the area. By 1845 the keels were disappearing, but still in use "on the Youghiogheny, the Monongahela above the improvement, [that is, above the dam] and other places inaccessible to steamboats." As late as June, 1862, the Cincinnati *Commercial* said: "The keelboatmen have it their own way on the Allegheny again, as it is entirely too low for steamboats."

The first mention of regular keelboat packets for freight and passengers on the Monongahela is in the Pittsburgh *Gazette* of September 2, 1786, when John Blair announced weekly boat service between Pittsburgh and points as far as 35 miles upriver. Later on there were several packet lines organized and running on a schedule which was pretty reliable, although subject of course to an upset of the timetable when the upstream-bound keels had to fight the current of a fresh or of seasonal high water or cope with unusually low water. It was sometimes necessary to cordelle over the riffles, a process so slow and so lacerating to the nerves that one wonders today how they put up with it. This consisted of running a double line out ahead and making it fast to some shore point, then twisting the line with capstan bars and thus drawing the boat upstream at a deadly slow pace.

Chapter 5

First Steamboat on Western Waters and Why

In 1807 Fulton and company launched the steamer *Clermont*. Although Rumsey, and Evans, and Stevens, and poor old Fitch, and a lot of other inventors had demonstrated that a boat could be moved through the water by steam power, Fulton and his partners had the cash and that's what makes the steamboats go. (It still does.) And so educational authorities are still teaching that Fulton "invented" the steamboat and no amount of correction from those who know seems to change this order of things.

The most amazing part of the story of steamboating in this country is the fact that only four years after the launching of the *Clermont* in 1807, away out in the interior of the country as then settled, in an atmosphere decidedly primitive and remote, men built another steamboat, which on its maiden voyage logged no less than two thousand miles on rivers obstructed by numberless bars, rapids, quixotic channels, and a chilling variety of snags, sawyers, deadheads, and rocks. And here is the way all that came about.

FIGURE 3. THE *New Orleans*, FIRST STEAMBOAT ON THE WESTERN
RIVERS, 1811.

In the first place, Rumsey fooled around with the steamboat idea but never got much of anyplace. Oliver Evans made a steamboat in 1804 that would run. John Stevens built five, between 1802 and 1806. William Longstreet built a steamboat that ran five miles an hour on the Savannah in 1790. In 1792 Elijah Ormsby of Connecticut operated a "side-paddle" steamboat. Samuel Morey built a paddle-wheel steamboat in 1794 and ran it from Hartford to New York City. In 1797 he built another one.

Fitch, however, actually had a steamboat running and "carrying passengers for hire" on the Delaware during the summer and fall of 1790. Everything went well until the company ran into legal trouble and Fitch, unable to get continued financial support, failed. Fitch made a few more tries, even went to France to build steamboats under the French laws. He almost made a go of it but ran into another streak of hard times. He finally went out to Kentucky, where he bucked his luck a few more years and then killed himself.

Actually, "at least sixteen steamboats had been launched in America before the building of the *Clermont*, fifteen of which had previously been operated under their own power by the eight different men who had designed them." In Europe there had been similar activity. As Louis C. Hunter states in his conclusive treatise called *Steamboats on the Western Rivers:* "The steamboat, like practically every mechanical complex of importance, was the product of many men working with a common heritage of technical knowledge and equipment and impelled by a common awareness of need." These words should be carved on the façade of every grammar school in our land.

Fulton was a rich man, and so were his partners. They were able to summon all the best talent available—the best steam engineers, the best boatbuilders, the best press agent—and of course the best of materials from timber to bell rope.

And it was Fulton who had the really bold idea of launching a boat on the western waters, while the *Clermont* was actually still in the test stages of operation as we would consider them today. Away out on the Monongahela, which he had never seen, he launched the *New Or-*

leans and thus brought the steamboat to the wild western waters probably years before it would have got there if left to the imaginations of others or to the inexorable but often deadly slow course of natural events. It is strange how slowly the use of many important inventions has spread from the little pinpoints on the map where they were born to the far-off places where they were needed. William Murdock, for example, invented gaslighting in 1791, and lighted his house and offices in Cornwall with it for several years before he could get anyone interested in the idea. And Andrew Carnegie, a boy from the Allegheny River bottoms who went into the steel business, and was considered quite successful by his neighbors, at first rejected the idea of the Bessemer converter as "newfangled."

But Fulton was a promoter. No sooner had the steam-propelled paddle-wheel boat been proved than he itched to startle the Indians of the west with a view of it, and in addition the prospect of holding a monopoly of steam propulsion on the entire Mississippi system tickled his fancy. It undoubtedly appealed also to his business partner, Robert R. Livingston, another prominent man of the day who valued gold and silver coins, bank notes, promissory notes, sight drafts, et cetera.

Fulton and Livingston required a man to survey the situation across the mountains, report on the prospects and possibilities in all their minute details, including local facilities for building a steamboat, and chances for commercial success. For this critical undertaking they admitted to the firm a junior partner, one Nicholas J. Roosevelt, who was sent to Pittsburgh in 1809 to size up the situation.

Roosevelt was at that time in possession of a brand new bride, who went along for the trip.

On arriving at Pittsburgh Roosevelt purchased a typical flatboat of the day, possibly from Stephen Bayard at "Elizabeth Town, on the Monongahela," who as early as 1788 was advertising in the Philadelphia papers that "Kentucky boats of different dimensions are available at as low a price as any on these waters."

At any rate, the honeymooners made the entire survey trip from Pittsburgh to the Lower Mississippi with apparent enjoyment, being in the capable hands of a pilot, three deckhands, and a cook (male). That Roosevelt confidently expected to return shortly with a genuine smoke-belching steamboat is testified to by the fact that at one point along the river, near Cincinnati, he had a supply of coal mined and stored for the use of the future boat. They had an extremely interesting and at times no doubt exciting trip, and reported back to New York in due time. Nobody they had met along the Monongahela, Ohio, or Mississippi had had anything good to say about the chances of working upstream with a boat that "ran on wheels," but nonetheless Roosevelt, having seen what the *Clermont* and the other vessels they had built on the Hudson could do, recommended a steam invasion of the waters flowing into the Gulf of Mexico at the earliest possible date.

The earliest possible date was 1810, when Mr. and Mrs. Roosevelt returned to Pittsburgh to supervise the construction of a new steamboat and to get it in motion on the water with all speed. The keel was laid on the banks of the Monongahela and the hull was launched in March, 1811. All of the spring and summer was spent in fitting out the boat and installing the engines, which were made by Joseph Tustin, a well-known manufacturer of steam engines. So far as I can find out, nobody knows whether this was a stern-wheel or a side-wheel boat. One authority states that "the boat had a paddlewheel on each side, and it is practically assured that these were on a single shaft, extending across the boat." Another says anyone who thinks the *New Orleans* was a side-wheeler ought to check in at a psychiatrist's.

Whichever it was, it turned its wheel in a progressive and determined manner, and after it had made a trial trip up the Monongahela, the Pittsburgh *Gazette* of October 18, 1811, reported feebly on the first steamboat on the Mississippi system as follows: "With pleasure we announce that the steamboat lately built at this place by Mr. Roosevelt, from an experiment made on Tuesday last, fully answers the most sanguine expectations that were formed for her sailing."

The boat is said to have cost $38,000. On Sunday, October 20, 1811, the pilot called for a good head of steam, the deckhand turned her loose, and the epoch-making trip was on. She spread consternation and amazement down the Ohio Valley, as can well be imagined. One old-timer remembered her like this:

"We saw something, I knew not what, but supposed it was a sawmill from the working of the lever beam, making its slow but solemn progress with the current. We were afterwards informed that it was a steamboat."

At Cincinnati and Louisville there were celebrations, public receptions, grand balls, and banquets, complete with speeches. Owing to low water the falls at Louisville could not be negotiated, causing a delay of a month. In the interval Roosevelt ran the boat back up to Cincinnati, thus spiking the guns of the local know-it-alls who had been giving everybody the inside information that the boat would not go upstream.

Mrs. Roosevelt celebrated this triumph by having a baby when they got back to Louisville. The arrival of the baby no doubt served to convince any remaining doubting Toms that the steamboat was truly a remarkable invention, and definitely here to stay.

Reaching the Mississippi they ran into the great earthquake of 1811, which scrambled the channel completely and swallowed several islands. Nevertheless, they reached New Orleans in January, 1812, with all safe and in good order including the baby, and after more toasts and southern hospitality, the boat entered the New Orleans and Natchez trade, where she operated successfully until cut down and sunk by a snag two years later, in 1814.

Back on the Monongahela the success of this venture did not go unnoticed and other boats were built. The dawn-age steamboats (or Urdämpfer) on the western waters, all ten or twelve of them, *were built on the banks of the Monongahela River*. None operated on the stream of its birth but went south and west.

FIGURE 4. Rafts, Flatboats, and a Keelboat.

The second boat on western waters was the *Comet*, built at Brownsville in 1813 by Daniel French and Henry M. Shreve. This was a shrimp of a boat, only 25 tons. The same men then built the *Despatch*, also small, in 1814; the *Enterprise*, 75 tons, in 1814; and the *Washington*, 403 tons, in 1816. These boats were operated successfully in defiance of the Fulton "monopoly" and encouraged others to enter the steamboat business.

Meanwhile the Fulton group had built three more good-sized boats and placed them in operation in the west: *Vesuvius* (340 tons, 1814), *Aetna* (360 tons, 1815), and another *New Orleans* (324 tons, 1815).

Of all these boats, one clearly demonstrated the practicability of steam navigation on the Ohio and Mississippi. This was Henry Shreve's *Washington*, incorporating almost all the features which subsequently formed that ethereal creature of grace and beauty—the western river steamboat. Shreve made his boat flat bottomed, with shallow draft. He hauled the machinery up out of the hold, improved it and placed it on deck where it belongs. He also built an upper deck. There is some argument among historians as to whether all these innovations appeared in the *Washington* or in subsequent vessels built by Shreve but, one way or another, he gets the credit. And it was definitely his famous trip in the *Washington*, upstream from New Orleans to Louisville in 1817, that "convinced the despairing public that steamboat navigation would succeed on the western waters."

By 1820 the boom was on and the steamboat builders of the Monongahela and the Ohio were going strong.

All the trunk lines of the river system had operating steam-boats, and by 1830 steamboating had extended west to include nearly all the tributaries of the Mississippi. The pageant of the packets had begun.

Chapter 6

From the Golden Triangle to the Old Tygart

Now if we enter the Monongahela from the Ohio, passing the Golden Triangle on the port side, and start upstream, we enter immediately into an area jampacked with human beings, commercial enterprises, and statistics. You can't any more get away from statistics than you can get away from the hum of industry and progress that fills that rich and wonderful valley from brim to brim. Everything is the "oldest," the "biggest," the "first west of the Alleghenies," or "was built at a cost of 33,000,000,000 dollars." All these statistics are not to be ignored, and besides, the towns that stand here on the banks of the ancient Monongahela have a rare flavor of their own, composed as they are of a blend of history, and Pennsylvania custom, old houses, old walls, old names, and a dynamic, part-European, modern culture.

Going upstream through Pittsburgh, especially at night, is an amazing experience. We are surrounded by the smoke and uproar of 62 glass factories, 350 coal mines, and 35 steel mills, plus uncountable other noisy enterprises, all blamming away. As we start up the historic river we go under the Point Highway Bridge, then the Smithfield Street Highway Bridge (this bridge is on the site of the earliest bridge across the Monongahela), and then the bridges come thick and fast and we are dodging the big coal-laden barge fleets of Jones & Laughlin, Union Barge Line, Carnegie-Illinois, and Hillman, not to mention small craft, a possible dredge or two, sand and gravel rigs, push boats and skiffs, all seeming about to run afoul of each other. By daytime, the eye can wander over the roofs of mill, factory, and warehouse, to the curiously varied architectural exhibits of the hillsides (stained glass, golden oak, "art brick," faded wedding cake, peeling Ruskinesque, Pittsburgh Gothic, steeltown Romanesque, nightmare Victorian, 1895 "modernistic," 1923 Sears Roebuck, steamboat colonial—cupolas, turrets, lace-curtain bay windows, cement block, tier after tier of turn-of-the-century balloon frame realtors' errors, and always the "rowhouses," smoke begrimed, flat faced, clinging precariously to the steep slopes), always the tunnels, inclines, long steep flights of wooden stairs, and always the pattern of skyscraper, tower, and church steeple rising above the dingy secrets of Pittsburgh's riches and fame.

In these smoky precincts many wonderful things have taken place, and not in steel and coal and bank deposits only, for long associated with the brutal city of raw realities are the names of such creative artists as Willa Cather, Hervey Allen, Mary Roberts Rinehart, Malcolm Cowley, George and Gilbert Seldes, Marc Connelly, Robinson Jeffers, Gertrude Stein, and John Kane (primitive painter of coal towns, tipples, and postcard views of Monongahela-land), and Mary Cassatt, and Ethelbert Nevin, Victor Herbert, and Stephen Collins Foster. Out of the grime, and smell of slag, and glow of nighttime blast furnaces came poems and songs and paintings.

It was thus from the earliest times in Pittsburgh. "After the revolutionary war," says H. M. Brackenridge (whose father was one of the prominent citizens of early times), "a number of families of the first respectability, principally of officers of the army, were attracted to this spot, and hence a degree of refinement, elegance of manners and polished society, not often found in the extreme frontier. The Butlers, the O'Haras, the Craigs, the Kirk-patricks, the Stevensons, the Wilkinses, the Nevilles, are names which will long be handed down by tradition." The town was the key to the West, frequently if not constantly visited by travelers of distinction, who usually tarried a few days on the point between the rivers making preparations for the trip west, and thus lent peculiar character and unusual interest to the place.

Although maligned the world over for its sooty flavor, Pittsburgh has always been a recognizable force in American progress in the arts and sciences. In medicine, way back in the sixties, Dr. A. M. Pollack was experimenting with the use of the wire loop as a substitute for the ligature in amputation. Today there are the Mellon Institute, the William H. Singer Memorial Laboratories, and the Institute of Pathology. In the art world of America today, no prize is more significant than the Carnegie award.

On the starboard side, Homestead is the first community we come to on our upstream voyage, a soot-coated town of 20,000 people and 100,000 smog-smeared windowpanes. Here in 1881, Carnegie started his Pittsburgh-Bessemer Steel Company, now one of the largest units in United States Steel Corporation. The most widely known incident in Homestead's history was the 1892 steel strike. This was not so much a strike as a shooting war waged by three hundred Pinkerton detectives hired by H. C. Frick against the striking union. In the attempt to dislodge the strikebreakers from a barge in the Monongahela from which they had planned to enter the plant, the strikers used burning oil, gas, dynamite, pistol and cannon fire. The plants eventually reopened on the company's terms. The strike has been so much discussed by labor leaders and students of labor problems that it has become a standard narrative in texts for the histories of American labor. The furor it caused over the nation at the time was loud, strenuous, and bitter.

Homestead was originally called "Amity Homestead."

The borough of Munhall is next to Homestead. The first openhearth furnace in the United States was opened here in 1886. This is a nice town with wide streets, and a rambling casual plan. The famous Queen Aliquippa sold 327 acres here in 1786 for assorted plunder worth about $260. This real estate has increased in value considerably since the time of the queen but the air has lost some of its quality.

Across the river at the other end of the two highway bridges and the Union Railroad Bridge are the towns of Rankin and Braddock. Rankin is a typical steel town of row-houses rising up a hill beside the river, the chief feature of the neighborhood being a mill called the Carrie Furnace. The Carrie Furnace stretches for a mile along the river and has little to recommend it to the eye of the aesthete. It employs 1,000 workers, some of whom, being Slavs, Italians, Serbs, Greeks, and members of other effervescent racial stocks, rise to prominence from time to time in many fields of intellect or emotion.

Next door to Rankin is Braddock, named of course for General Braddock. Within its present city limits the defeat of his British and colonial troops took place at the hands of the French and Indians in 1755. The slaughter itself is supposed to have occurred in the neighborhood of Jones and Bell Avenues. Braddock is another steel and iron town; but to add a note of variety it also boasts a "wall plaster factory."

In Duquesne, which is laid out on the inside of the next bend south of Braddock and across the river, the story is again steel. The Carnegie-Illinois plant here produces 136,000 tons of ingot steel and 1,000,000 tons of bar steel every year.

Across the river, at the mouth of the Youghiogheny River, is McKeesport, settled in 1755 by David McKee, a North Country Irishman, who ran one of the first Monongahela ferries at this point. Up the Youghiogheny, Henry Overholt may be said to have invented rye whisky. He was a weaver, a Bucks County Mennonite, who moved into the region about 1800 and in tending the family still made so many improvements in the distillation process that he erected a distillery to capitalize on the fine whisky he had developed. The distillery originally had a daily output of 200 gallons.

McKeesport has a very large foreign-born population and the onion-shaped tops of the Russian church are seen here as elsewhere in the Monongahela Valley. In the shops and stores, in the movies and taverns, you hear the romantic music of foreign tongues, Italian, Czech, Russian, Greek, Polish, and some unidentifiable, but all giving the town a pleasant international air.

McKeesport is sometimes known as the Tube City, because the National Tube Company, "the largest of its kind in the world," has its factory here. The American Sheet and Tin Plate Company is also "the biggest," and the Firth-Sterling mill the "first fabricator of stainless steel in America."

In 1794 McKeesport was a center in the local disturbance, target practice, and barn burning known as the Whisky Rebellion. An attempt was made in early times to engineer a slack-water system on the Youghiogheny, but the dams washed out in the raging spring floods and the project was given up. Boatbuilding began very early here, and the history of the town is intimately connected with the river.

Incidentally they had a hell of a time over at East McKeesport at the time of the big snowstorm in November, 1950. This was the worst snowfall in the history of the Pittsburgh area—28 inches. Anyway, at East McKeesport, which is the gateway to the Pennsylvania state superhighway, there were a thousand stranded motorists. Their abandoned cars, trucks, and buses sprawled through the streets and on the roads leading into town, buried completely in giant drifts. The citizens of the town turned everything over to the unwilling guests and the firehouses, churches, and movie theaters were filled with refugees.

A couple of miles upriver is Glassport, where the glassworks at the foot of Seventh Street produces 15,000 different items of ordinary staple glassware. Let's see now . . .

Passing Coal Valley on the right and heading up on Bellbridge Light we pass another rugged industrial concentration, Clairton, distinguished by "the largest by-product coke plant in the United States." This was a peaceful residential town until the gay nineties, when the blight of industry fell upon it, and since then it has been glassworks, brickyards, steel mills, coke plants, and smoke. This coke plant covers 175 acres along two miles of river front and when I last asked, it had 1,134 ovens in 18 batteries.

Elizabeth, Pa., is upriver a little distance and across from Clairton; and although the population is only about three thousand, you certainly hear a lot about it on the river. It's one of the very oldest of the Monongahela towns, and was the scene of tremendous boatbuilding activities starting as far back as 1778. Later on, when steamboats came to the western waters, Elizabeth was one of the most important boatbuilding centers in the country. Monongahela history oozes out of the cracks in the sidewalks of this ancient town.

Today the Pittsburgh Consolidation Coal Company

operates the Elizabeth Marine Ways, about a quarter of a mile below the bridge, offering complete repairs to tow-boats—hull, engines, and equipment. If your towboat is in need of an overhaul call telephone number 63, Elizabeth, and ask for W. C. Kelly.

On the bluff just below Lock No. 3 at Elizabeth stands the residence of the late Captain John L. Howder, who died in 1951. Captain Howder began his river career in 1890 at the age of 13 as cabin boy and won his captain's license at the age of 21. He was captain of the *Helen White* of the United Coal Company when she was sold to Mexican interests for use on the Panuco River at the time of the Tampico oil strike and he took her across the Gulf of Mexico himself, something few rivermen ever attempted.

The industrial uproar quiets down a bit as we proceed upriver beyond Clairton and Elizabeth. Then a few miles up we come to Monongahela, where the clangor is heard again; Donora, on the big bend in the river, whose local mill produces "the largest tonnage of wire in the world;" Monessen, more steel, coal, and smoke; Charleroi, glass, glass, and more glass; and on past Bellevernon, Little Redstone Creek, the Republic Steel Tipple, and around hairpin Greenfield Bend, the J. & L. Tipple at California, Warren Elsey Light, Redstone Creek, and so under the Pennsylvania Railroad Bridge and into Brownsville.

You would never think, to walk the streets of Browns-ville today, that the town is old and filled with history and legend. Monongahela Valley towns just do not look the part as do Lexington and Concord and Portsmouth and

Gloucester and Boston and Philadelphia. For famous Redstone Old Fort, now Brownsville, is another "industrial town," and aside from the Greek Revival, post-Colonial Playford House on Second and Market Streets, little romance is visible.

Colonel James Burd selected the site of Redstone Old Fort in 1758 because of the presence there of an early Indian fortification, and built his stockade. In 1785 Thomas and Basil Brown founded the town, which in the years to follow played an important part in the westward movement. It was at Brownsville that the weary emigrants saw the end of their toilsome struggle over the mountains and took to the calm waters of the Monongahela for the next lap of their journey. As the steamboat rose to fame and fortune on the western waters and industrial activity in the valley grew, the Brownsville-Pittsburgh trade developed. Even before the slack-water system had been completed to Brownsville in 1844, there were about two hundred steamboat arrivals annually at Pittsburgh from upriver points. After the locks and dams went into service, there was a daily packet line between Pittsburgh and Brownsville.

There is an old iron bridge in Brownsville that I inspected one time when we were laid up in drydock out at the Hillman shipyard. This bridge is on Market Street near Bank, and it has a tablet on it which says it is the first iron bridge west of the Alleghenies. It was apparently built in the period 1836-1839 of iron forged in local furnaces. Before this bridge was built, Henry Clay's carriage overturned near this spot, dumping the great man into Dunlap's Creek. They say that Clay "gathered himself up with the remark that Clay and mud should not be mixed in that place again." Clay then returned to Washington to his senator's post and shortly afterwards an order was issued for the construction in Brownsville of an "iron span, carrying the road high above the stream."

After we go under the Brownsville Highway Bridge, height 50.2 feet above low water, span 386 feet, we come to Dam 5, and after locking through, we pass the Alicia Marine Ways of the Hillman Company and then are pretty much out in the country, except for coal mines and tipples at regular intervals. There's Vesta tipple and Frick Mine Light, Fox Mine Light and the H. C. F. Coke Company tipple, Vestaburg and Fredericktown and the bend around to Tenmile Creek, and Emerald Tipple, Pumpkin Run, Klein's Sawmill Light, Crucible Fuel Company tipple, and Light, Weirton Steel Company tipple, National Steel Corporation Pier, Buckeye Coal Company tipple, Browns Run, Little Whiteley Creek, Robena Mine Light and tipple, Pittsburgh Steel tipple, Duquesne Light Company tipple, Jacobs Creek, and then around the bend to Dam 7.

Below Dam 7 are Greensboro on the starboard side, and New Geneva on port. New Geneva boasts a population of 410 souls, more or less, and was named for the native city of its famous early settler, Albert Gallatin. Gallatin came to this country without friends or influence, and by the sheer power of his personality and ability (and despite the handicap of a monumental French accent) achieved appointment as a member of the President's

Cabinet within ten years of his arrival. A man of many talents, Gallatin served in the Revolutionary War, then became a French instructor at Harvard. Later he journeyed to Richmond on business and there became an intimate of Governor Patrick Henry, who advised him to go west to the wild lands of opportunity out by the Monongahela.

Gallatin settled in Fayette County, a few miles from New Geneva and in a short time established the first glassworks west of the Alleghenies. In 1789 he built Friendship Hill, a 2½-story, ivy-covered residence, still standing and open to the public. He began to enter local politics, filling several state and federal posts, and in 1801 was appointed secretary of the treasury by President Jefferson. He served in this post during both of Jefferson's presidential terms, the whole of President Madison's first term, and until February, 1814, in the second, something of a record in Cabinet tenure. After retirement from the Cabinet this energetic adopted son of the new Republic held several diplomatic posts and finally, between 1831 and 1839 was president of the National Bank of New York.

Patrick Henry said Albert Gallatin was one of the most extraordinary men he had ever seen. He was surely of keen intellectual powers and magnificent ability in political and diplomatic affairs—the model statesman.

At Friendship Hill the dignified retirement of Gallatin was embellished in 1825 by a visit from "his long tried, his bosom friend," the Marquis de Lafayette. Of this sumptuous affair an old Monongahelite, James Veech (writing in 1858), said: "Who that was there can ever forget the 'feast of reason'—and other good things,

FIGURE 5. MONONGAHELA-BUILT DEEP-SEA SAILING VESSELS DRIFTING TO SEA.

and the 'flow of soul'—and champagne? The like of which old Springhill [Township] had never seen—may never see again."

In the five miles upriver from New Geneva to Point Marion, where the Cheat River enters the Monongahela, no less than five coal tipples are busy dumping Pennsylvania coal into waiting barges. Point Marion has a large glassworks and a sand and gravel company which owns a baby Diesel towboat with a steam boiler for operating the steering rig and blowing the whistle, a quaint arrangement unique in my experience.

Around a few bends and beyond more tipples, Morgantown rises on the hills to port. Ah, Morgantown, with your glass factories and coal mines and spaghetti at Capellanti's and houses all peeling from chemical fumes in the air! On Saturday nights in spring the boys and girls from the University of West Virginia, perched up on the hill at the end of Main Street, mingle on the sidewalks down by the courthouse with coal miners and farmers and glassworkers. To us on the *Coal Queen*, Morgantown was everything, our metropolis—the hot bath, the glass of Tube City beer, the lump-in-throat in the movies, the Girl, paradise, purgatory—we knew them all in Morgantown. But Morgantown knew little of us. Steamboaters, with their excitable and noisy ways, are not invited to tea parties. I can call every bartender and short-order waitress in town by name but the mayor and I have yet to shake hands.

Above Morgantown the Monongahela is a beautiful narrow stream running between high hills—"mountains," we always called them. The locks are small, the traffic is light, and there is a friendly intimacy between boat crews and lock tenders. The locks are so close that in a six-hour watch you might make seven or eight locks. After a few months of this, running those locks seemed automatic. That's pretty country up in there from Morgantown to National Mine, and pretty again above Jordan, especially in the spring, when the trees and flowers are all in bloom. And then, half blinded sometimes by the smoke from the railroad yard, we come to Fairmont, and beyond it the "Dark Bridge" (no lights on it), which we all hated, and then there was the point, where the Monongahela ended, a point with a big tree on it, a good mark and easy to pick up with the searchlight on a bad night.

The Monongahela is formed by the West Fork River and the Tygart River, which join here at Fairmont, 128.73 miles south of Pittsburgh. The tipple where we loaded coal was at Kingmont, up the Tygart, two miles above head of navigation on the Monongahela, and we would snake our loads out of there in a river so narrow you could nearly jump across.

Now just imagine, in the old days you could take a good big steamboat from Fairmont, West Virginia, at the headwaters of the Monongahela, down to Cairo, up the Mississippi and Missouri to Fort Benton, Mont.—3,623 miles, or about as far as from the North River in New York to the East India Docks on the Thames at London. In fact the stern-wheeler *E. H. Durfee* made *regular trips* between Pittsburgh and Fort Benton in the years 1872 to 1876. Wouldn't that be something, to raise steam amidst the roar of industry on the Monongahela and keep that paddle wheel splashing until you began to run into buffalo and Sioux and the Rocky Mountains?

Chapter 7

Locks and Shipyards
Along the Mon

Boatbuilding on the Monongahela began with the craft built by the members of the French garrison at Fort Duquesne in the 1750's and has never stopped. Improving the bottom, sides, and surface of the Monongahela River itself started before 1800 and is still going on.

First about the locks.

The history of the "improvement" of the Mononga-hela is long and in places dull and filled with bond issues and charters and petitions and protests and re-organizations and financial nightmares. At any rate, Locks 1 and 2 opened up for business in 1841, and although afflicted in 1843 by financial calamities, the Monongahela Navigation Company opened Locks 3 and 4 in the fall of 1844 when slack-water navigation between Pittsburgh and Browns-ville became a fact. According to the chief engineer's report for 1845, the locks were 190 by 50 feet, made of cut-stone masonry set in hydraulic cement and the gates were opened and closed with hand capstans. These mammoth locks were considered a wonder in those times, and great was the praise lavished on their builders.

In May, 1951, we read a news article by Captain Frederick Way, Jr., describing the newest Monongahela River lock as follows: "The Monongahela River is to have the largest lock, in linear dimensions, on inland rivers.[Since Captain Way wrote this, a larger lock is building on the Cumberland River and another at Chain of Rocks.] The chamber will be 720 feet long by 110 feet wide. This lock, which will be bigger than any on the Ohio River, Upper Mississippi or elsewhere, will modernize the plant at Lock Two, Braddock, Pa., located 11 miles above Pittsburgh. Two and a half years will be required to do the work. The 720-foot lock will be built on the shoreward side, and during its construction all traffic will pass through the new 360-foot structure. The completion of this enormous project will mean that standard Monongahela River tows, hitched 'three long, two wide' can be brought out from Brownsville, Pa., without breaking tow or without unfacing the towboat from the tow, a distance of 56.5 miles. Locks three and four, located respectively at Elizabeth, Pa., and Monessen, Pa., already have 720-foot chamers, 56 feet wide."

Locks 5 and 6 were added in the 1850's, bringing navigation to New Geneva. In 1879 the federal government for the first time took an active part and constructed Lock 9 (don't ask me what happened to Locks 7 and 8; they got lost in the shuffle, I guess, at least *I* have lost track of them) at Hoard's Rocks just inside the West Virginia state line and right up on the edge of the *Coal Queen* country. Finally the government took over the whole works (years of legal squabbles involved) and put in Locks 10 to 15 and extended navigation to Fairmont and even up the headwaters into the Tygart River at Kingmont. The sites of the various locks have been moved about so much in the past century that any discussion of them results in wild confusion, for, you see, Old Lock 3 was almost two miles above Elizabeth, and Old Lock 4 was at West Charleroi, about a half mile below the present one, whereas New Lock 2 was moved downstream for about one-half mile to Braddock, and of course Old Lock 11 is gone since New Lock 10 is completed and the improvement at New Lock 2 will result in its being called New New Lock 2.

Here's a good one: When the Post Office Department put out a two-cent stamp in 1929 to commemorate the completion of the Lock and Dam system on the Ohio River they had a nice picture on it of a lock with a steamboat locking through. The lock portrayed for the glorification of the Ohio River Valley is Lock 5 on the Monongahela River and the boat is Carnegie Steel Company's sternwheel steamer *H. D. Williams*, locking down through from the H. C. Frick mines on October 4, 1920, with a big tow of Monongahela coal.

What kind of tonnage do these locks handle? Well, they handle more tonnage than the Panama Canal, or the Kiel Canal, or the Suez Canal, or the Bruges Ship Canal, or the Kronstadt Canal, or the Trollhätte, Ghent-Terneuzen, Corinth, Hammarby, Marseille-Rhône, and Cape Cod canals—in fact more tonnage than any canal or canalized river in the world except the St. Mary's Falls Canal at Sault Ste. Marie. In the week ending January 20,

1951, for example, a total of 424,730 tons passed through Lock 3.

Now about boatbuilding. The most bizarre aspect of Monongahela boatbuilding was the period during which seagoing vessels were built, launched, loaded with cargo, and sent down the long river trail to salt water. This curious business was begun in 1801 when a number of farmers in the vicinity of Elizabeth (then Elizabethtown) organized a stock company and built the *Monongahela Farmer*, a deep-water schooner of 92 tons burden. The vessel was loaded with 721 barrels of flour, 500 barrels of rye whisky, 4,000 deerskins, 2,000 bearskins, plus some quantities of hemp, flax, and firearms. She left downbound with the above cargo in command of Captain John Walker, who was under the following orders from the owners:

"Proceed to New Orleans. Should the markets for flour be low at New Orleans and the vessel appear to sell at a disadvantage, you in that case have it in your power to sell a part of the cargo, to purchase rigging, fit out the vessel and employ hands to sail her to any of the Islands you in your Judgment and to the best information may think best, and then make sale of the vessel and cargo."

I wonder what a river captain of today would think of those orders. Nowadays the boat is in touch with the home office twice a day via radio-telephone and the captain consults the despatcher before he changes to a clean shirt, much less taking it on himself to find a purchaser and make a sale on favorable terms of not only a mixed cargo of commodities but the boat itself!

The *Monongahela Farmer* departed on a June rise, was stalled three months at the falls at Louisville, was attacked by Indians, lost a man overboard, stuck tight for several weeks on Walkers Bar above Hurricane Island, and finally reached New Orleans, where Captain Walker promptly sold cargo and schooner, took to bed with yellow fever, of which he almost died, but bounced back again, and arrived back home on the Monongahela after an absence of fourteen months with a profit for the farmer shipping magnates. He immediately superintended the building of the brig *Ann Jane*, a really good-sized vessel of 450 tons, loaded her up with more Monongahela rye and extra-fine flour, again sailed to New Orleans, but this time didn't stop—went right on out into the Gulf in this craft built more than two thousand miles from salt water and sailed her to New York, where he again sold at a nice profit. The *Monongahela Farmer* meantime had come around to New York for new owners, and was a regular trader out of that port for many years, breaking all records for speed in a run from New York to Balize.

The building of ships continued at other shipyards on the Monongahela, and in the Pittsburgh *Gazette* of January 21, 1803, we read this amazing notice: "Sailed, on Sunday last [16th] from this place *for Liverpool, England*, the brig DEAN, burthen 170 tons. She takes a cargo of cotton at the mouth of the Cumberland River, on freight, by Messrs. Meeker, Denman & Company, merchants of Philadelphia."

In his edition of the 1817 *Navigator* Uncle Zadok says: "Misfortunes and accidents in getting [deep-water vessels] down the Ohio, which most probably arose from bad management in the persons entrusted with them, has given a damp to ship-building, and it is now transferred to steam boat building." I think he is implying that the persons entrusted with the ships were too tight to turn loose of a dollar for a copy of the *Navigator* and hence wrecked what could have been a thriving industry.

The true history of nineteenth-century steamboat building on the banks of the Monongahela is a subject bigger than Texas. We give here only a few notes.

Brownsville was the oldest and most important center of steamboat building on the Monongahela; after one hundred and forty-some years they are still building steamboats at Brownsville, or anyway they advertise "all types of river craft." They would no doubt build you a genuine steam-propelled boat if you wanted one, positively insisted on it; otherwise they are engaged in building high-powered screw-propeller river towboats equipped with dreary Diesel engines and some infernal device called a Kort nozzle. Trouble is they let a bunch of these boys from the State College with slide rules into the shipyards and good-bye you fuel-wasting, inefficient, impractical, incompetent, infeasible, infernal, inflammable, and beautiful steamboats.

Other prominent yards on the smoky shores of the Monongahela were those at Pittsburgh, of course, and at Elizabeth, Bellevernon, McKeesport, West Elizabeth, Port Perry, Monongahela City, Webster, Fayette City, West Newton (up the Youghiogheny), and the records even show that a steamboat was built and launched up at Morgantown! At the Walker yards in Elizabeth the *J. M. White* was built in 1844, "probably" the fastest steamboat that ever turned a wheel on the Mississippi system. At California, Pa., in 1855 the comical *Kate Frisbee* was built. She was disassembled at New Orleans and shipped around Cape Horn to San Francisco for use on the Sacramento River. She arrived in the middle of a rate war on that river and the warring factions bought off her owners, who promptly shipped her *back* around Cape Horn again, put her together again and ran her on the Mississippi.

Oh, there were actually hundreds of famous boats built on the Monongahela. Way up the little shallow tributaries of the far west, up in the country of the Big Sky, and down in the spooky bayous draped with Spanish moss —everywhere that steamboats ran, and they ran nearly anyplace where there was water enough to float a shingle in those days—you could find a Monongahela-built steamboat! And as the century wore along the boatbuilders from Pittsburgh to Brownsville and on down the Ohio evolved the beauteous creature compounded of white oak, poplar, white pine, boiler plate, cast iron, paint, glass, gilt, poetry and music which we remember as the Western River Steamboat. Somehow or other American steamboat architecture resulted in a finished form of great elegance, balance, and subtle grace—amazing when you consider the majority of the county courthouses of the period. And along with the aesthetic perfection of the steamboat came mechanical improvements: the steam whistle, the steam capstan or "nigger," the "doctor" pump, the Lyman Patent steam gauge, the Bourdon bent tube gauge, wrought-iron boiler heads and steam pipes, glass tube water gauges, and a fine array of innovations in valves, all testifying to the progressive energy expended on the steamboat. In the 1850's somebody invented or introduced or otherwise brought forth the steam calliope and set it up on the hurricane deck, and the steamboat reached the ripe blossoming point of her voluptuous young womanhood.

Alas, poor girl, the winter rain has been pelting the legend on her headstone these many years. Like all beings of youth and charm and careless rapture, she went to the grave and her boilers are as cold as the tomb.

Chapter 8

The Wonderful Day

Once upon a time on the Upper Monongahela River there was a Wonderful Day. This happened in spring and it was the kind of a day when the old folks remember how wonderful they were when they were young, and the young folks think of how wonderful they'll be when they're older. The sun was gently soothing Roast as he lay napping on the deck beside the galley door, the bees were buzzing in the long grass at Flaggy Meadow, and the air, if not like wine, was at least like Budweiser. And on this Wonderful Day the mighty motor vessel *Coal Queen* ran hard aground below Lock 13, coming downriver with one load.

We locked through and were just clear of the gates when we suddenly stopped. We were stuck fast. It was about ten in the morning and I was off watch and sound asleep. But so sensitive (or so ridiculous) are the emotions of the steamboat maniac that I became uneasy and soon awoke. We were not in a lock, I could tell that. And we weren't making a landing. Something special was up, something was happening to break the ding-dong monotony of this coal run. There were shouts on deck, and great activities in the engine room, with many stops and starts of the engine. What riverman could lie in the sack with such evidences of excitement clattering through the boat?

"What's the matter, Duke?" I said as I went into the pilothouse.

"Not a thing. We are merely hard aground and it looks like we'll stay that way," he said.

We busted the boat loose and tried shoving on the head of the load. We shoved on the other side. We took soundings. We drank a lot of coffee and smoked a lot of cigarettes. The deckhands offered theories. Roast volunteered the thought that "them boys at the tipple loaded her lobsided." National blamed the company.

After an hour of fruitless bumping and shoving we dumped the yawl in the river and Duke and I rowed over to shore and walked up to the lockhouse. After a palaver with the lockmaster we persuaded him to call the Grafton dam upriver and ask them to open the gates and send some water down.

"Now that's more like it," Duke said. "When you reckon that water'll get here?"

"Oh, let's see. It's eleven A.M." says the lockmaster. "Oughta get a rise down here about nine or ten o'clock tonight."

"So long, kid," Duke said. "I'll go over the mountain road and report to the company."

"Why not telephone from here?" I said.

"Don't be so worrisome, Beedle," he said. "I'll see you when you get down to Morgantown."

What a mighty captain! So there I was, with the whole outfit stuck fast, and the captain gone to town to "report." My, but he was in some hurry to get there and "report." This old Duke was a prize for a captain, all right. The Responsibility of Command, the Company's Interest, and the Stern Ethics of the Marine Profession were as so many soap bubbles to him. In all my wanderings over the watery surface of the world, in deep and shallow water, from Beirut to Sioux City, I never met a captain like our Duke.

So I rowed back to the boat and the chief Engineer was out on the guard and he spits into the river. "Where's Duke?" he says.

"He went over the mountain," I said. "He claims he's going to town and report our troubles."

"Report to that Irene is all the report he's gonna make," he says. "Well, are they gonna send us down some water?"

"Yeah. The man says we'll have water about nine or ten tonight."

"My God, this will kill the company," he said. "They will have a fit to hear we sat around enjoying ourselves for ten whole hours."

"The captain don't seem a bit worried," I said.

"I bet he ain't," says the chief. Then he went back in the engine room. Then he stuck his head out. "You wanna work the engine any more?"

"No," I said. "Let her go. We'll warm her up about eight P.M. I'm gonna do something on this spring day I been wanting to do for three weeks."

"What's that?"

"Go swimming."

"I seen everything on the Union Barge Line and the Barrett Line and the West Kentucky Coal Company," he says. "I seen a captain drop dead. I seen two men scalded to death. I seen a lady cook stick a butcher knife clear through a deckhand's shoulder. But I never seen a pilot in swimmin' before."

"Stick around," I said. "Captain Darnell of the Royal Navy is gonna walk the high wire after I get through."

I went out on the barge and took off my clothes and set them on the deck on a newspaper and dove into the Monongahela. It was a little bit colder than I would have thought. After a winter in the bunkroom, if that river water didn't feel like home. I swam up alongside the boat and floated around on my back for a while looking up at the sky, as blue as calendar art.

"You'll get typhoid I bet," says the chief, looking out the engine-room door.

"Say, do you smile on Christmas Day?" I said.

The second engineer came out of the bunkroom. I thought for a minute he was about to give me some pointers on how to swim, but instead he took off his pants and jumped into the river.

"I thought you told me this water was all full of coal poisoning from the mines," I said. "I thought you said this river had all kinds germ bacterials in it."

"This time of year it ain't got so many," he says. "My, don't that water feel good."

Pretty soon National came out of the galley with two peanut butter sandwiches and a cup of coffee.

"Ain't that water kinda cold?" he says, and he sits down on the stern end of the barge, sets his coffee cup on a timberhead like he was at a tea party, and dangles his legs over the edge.

The second was idling around in the water alongside the barge and all of a sudden he grabs ahold of National's old dirty boot.

"Oh, it ain't bad," he says, and gives a big heave. The coffee cup flew up in the air, a peanut butter sandwich soared over my head, and National landed in the river with a grand big splash. Roast was sticking his head out the galley window and, my, how he did carry on.

"Dang fools," says the chief. "What a career I got for myself on this outfit."

Well, we swam around for quite a while, had a good purification in that mountain water, finally climbed out and got dressed. "Come on," I says to the second, "let's get up in them woods and do some herborizing."

"Good idea," he says. "What is it?"

"Looking for flowers and stuff," I says.

"I'm gonna get me a couple oranges, wait a minute," says the second.

We rowed ashore and tied up the yawl and climbed the bank. Weeks, years, centuries of coal barge and greasy plate and bunkroom were left behind as we plunged up through the fringe of meadow turning green, through the patches of violets spread under the hot spring sun. We got to the edge of the woods, and we entered into the shade of the tall timber, virgin timber.

"You know all about these here trees? What kind of a

tree is that?" the second said. He looked pale and unfamiliar in this strange setting.

"That's a beech, and that whopper over there is a white oak," I said. "And there's hickory, see that with the rough bark, and over yonder, there's a buckeye and a couple hard maples and, look, that big one with the fat round trunk, that's a black walnut tree. See the tall one way over there with the limb split off, that's cottonwood, you oughta see the size they grow to out west. Come on along, we ought to come into an open place up here, and if we do there'll be hawthorn and crabapples, they're the trees we used to see from the boat a while back, with the white blossoms and the pink ones."

"My God, where did you get all them names at?" the second said. He stopped and sat down. "My ain't it a change to get away from that boat to someplace besides a tavern? Lordy, lordy, why look, I'm settin' right on top of some flowers. Now what would you call this here, perfessor?" he said, handing me some little pink flowers.

"Why, that's trailing arbutus," I said. "Smell it, buddy, if you want a treat for your smeller. It's late for that to be blooming. But there's some orange azalea, see that, pretty, ain't it? That's *wild* azalea. Come on, excelsior a little bit, you got to climb, engineer, if you want to be a first-class herborizer."

We climbed up through more arbutus, and white anemone, through clouds of violets flung down in the fresh and spicy shade; we brushed aside trilliums, half ready to blossom, and crushed the golden ragwort under our rude mariner's boats. The zephyrs gently swished through the

FIGURE 6. THE *Kate Adams*, BUILT IN SEWICKLEY, PENNSYLVANIA, 1882. ENGINES BUILT BY DUQUESNE ENGINE WORKS ON THE MONONGAHELA.

lindens, poplars, and sweet gum trees, and a mockingbird deep in a hemlock gave us song.

"Listen, ain't that something?" said the second, who was born in a culvert and raised in a slum. "Funny the way them damn birds hang around out here in the woods singin', ain't it?"

Come to think of it, it is kind of a peculiar proposition. Raised in the country you take it for granted; but look at it again, and there isn't any sense to it at all. What the hell do they do it for anyway?

Finally we came to a big shelf of rock sticking right out into space with a clump of red cedars behind, and a great big oak tree towering above. And below, way down below us, was the river.

"God almighty, look at that," says the second. "Look, don't the river look funny down there? Damn! Look, there's the boat. Look how little she is!"

"Gimme a cigarette, engineer," I said. "Let's lie down and ease our weary steamboat bones. Let that West Virginia sun bake some health back into our poor pale cheeks."

"Sing 'em blues, kid," the second said, passing me a cigarette and matches. "Sing 'em blues, Mr. Pilot."

"We're fools, second," I said. "We're A-1 prime stock, clear grain fools. Now why in the name of sixty dollars didn't we scout around and bring some beer up here? I bet old locktender down there has got an icebox full of it."

"Ain't you never happy?" says second. "Can't you set here and enjoy yourself? Now you not only ruined your own pleasure but mine likewise. While you're at it wishin'

for beer why not wish for two dolls, a redhead and a bru-
nette?"

"How you gettin' along with your wife now?" I said.
He was a boy with his third wife already.

"Another swell topic. Since you ask, there ain't no
change. *And* she ain't sent me that bathrobe yet. I got a letter from the lawyer. Ashtabula lawyer. I wrote him back
I says tell that wife of mine when I gets that bathrobe then
come and talk about support. Ain't gonna talk about nothin' until I see that bathrobe. That's what I told her a
dozen times. Back in November I says to her when I wrote
I says, 'It's cold around the bunkroom on this boat and
please honey send my bathrobe via parcels post to c/o Box
18 Morgantown.' Here it is May now, and do you think she
sent me that robe yet? No. She's too busy, goin' to the picture show with that Lucille, and hangin' around over at
the drugstore. No, I ain't seen that robe of mine and she
ain't seen no money. Stubborn? Why, even that Ashtabula
lawyer can't get her to ship out that robe. He says they are
going to attack my salary. 'Just send my bathrobe,' I says
last time I wrote him, 'and you won't need to attack no
salary. But send the robe first.' "

A purple finch came and sat on one of the cedar trees.
A puff of breeze came down the mountainside and stirred
the shaded flowers.

"Well, what happened?"

"Nothin'. No robe. She is just bound and determined
not to send the robe. The lawyer he can't pry no robe
loose from her. I b'lieve that lawyer, old Prentiss or what-

ever his name is, I b'lieve he'd wrap it up and send it on himself if only she'd turn loose of it but not her. No. She ain't gonna send me no robe and, by God, she's there to see nobody else does either. Imagine a man to have such a woman with a bathrobe. Her and that robe has about got me licked. I admit it. I ain't ashamed to say so. Her and that robe has about got me licked."

The Wife, the Robe, and the Lawyer gathered around the second engineer, plucked him, poked him, grinned with hideous leers and demanded support. They chased him up and down the shaded alleys beneath the hardwood trees, they buried him in flowers, they stuck a dead finch in his pocket, they rolled him in the moss and ferns under a chinquapin tree, they tickled him with the three-toothed cinquefoil and stuffed his ears with phymosia and coltsfoot. "No robe!" screamed the wife. "Support!" cried the lawyer. "Never, never," whispered the robe, and it climbed to the top of the Mingo Oak and surveyed the wild Monongahela as far as the dark bridge and the Tygart Valley and the glacial bogs; through a brassbound telescope viewed the giant hawthorn and the carnivorous sundew. The wife rolled off the cliff. The Ashtabula lawyer opened his briefcase and offered beer. The engineer crawled under a root. Flowers burst into song and the trees split.

When I awoke the second was lying on his stomach looking over the edge of the rock. A black beetle was promenading up his trouser leg, creeping in and out of the patches of light and shade that patterned the dirty tan cotton twill. Way over the distant hills two hawks were wheeling against the blue. I put my red handkerchief over my face and fell asleep again.

The Wonderful Day ended at 10:00 P.M. that night. The water got down to us from up at the headwaters and the barge came loose and we shoved off down the river again. Up in the pilothouse of the motor vessel *Coal Queen* there was a milk bottle with a bunch of flowers stuck in it.

We picked up Duke at the landing at 1:00 A.M. and I went to bed. In the morning when I went on watch again the milk bottle and the flowers were gone, and the Wonderful Day was all gone too.

Chapter 9

The Black Stones

The *Encyclopaedia Britannica* says: "By coal is compre-
hended all the fossil fuels contained in the earth's crust."
Along the Monongahela coal is just plain coal and coal
rules the world.

"Coal, strictly speaking, is not a mineral but a rock,
and, further, it is a sedimentary rock; the mineral sub-
stance, consisting mainly of complex carbon compounds, is
amorphous," also says the Encyclopaedia.

Still don't know much about it. Any deckhand present know what "amorphous" means? Let's try again.

"There is no standard coal: there is an almost endless
series of varieties, from brown coal at the one extreme to
anthracite at the other."

That's one thing I never saw up the Monongahela,
brown coal. But I bet they have it.

"That the ancient Britons in general were acquainted
with coal as such is evident from its appellation at the present time, which is not Saxon but British, and subsists
among the Irish as *gual*, amongst the Cornish in *kolan*,
and in Welsh as *glo* to this day."

These facts should be transmitted at once to the Mine

Workers of America. There's hardly a miner at Rosedale or Booth that knows the Cornish appellation for coal.

"The first record of the use of coal in Great Britain is frequently stated [first time *I* ever heard it stated] to be A.D. 852, when it is recorded . . . that the Abbot Ceobred let the land of Sempringham to Wulfred, who was to send each year to the monastery '60 loads of wood, 12 loads of coal, 6 loads of peat, etc.' "

Anybody up the Monongahela with a name like Wulfred is under suspicion and has a hard time getting a drink.

Now listen to this:

"Coal is the outcome of a process of transformation whereby the oxygen and hydrogen contained in the woody fibre and other vegetable matter are eliminated in proportionally larger quantity than carbon, so that the percentage of the latter element is increased."

But cheer up, for actually:

". . . indeed, perhaps of all the problems connected with the natural history of coal we know least about the methods of its conversion, although the researches of B. Renault ("Sur quelques Micro-organismes des combustibles fossiles," *Bull. Soc. Indust. Miner.* Sér. 3, vol. xiii, p. 868, 1899; vol. xiv. p. 5, 1900, and "Recherchés sur les Bacteriacées fossiles," *Ann. Sci. Nat.*, Sér. 8, Bot. vol. ii, p. 275, 1896) have gone a long way toward helping us to an understanding of the processes involved in the transformation of the original vegetable matter into coal."

Now, coal in the Pittsburgh district is like corn in Iowa—it is all over the place. Even from the earliest times, coal was known and used for fuel. As Zadok Cramer says in the 1811 edition of his *Navigator* (which was sort of a flatboatmen's Blue Book of the Allegheny, Monongahela, and Ohio): "The hills of the Allegheny and Monongahela rivers are filled with good coal mines up to their head waters. A coal mine was opened in 1760, opposite to Fort Pitt on the Monongahela, for the use of that garrison . . . Pittsburgh has long been celebrated for its coal banks, and both as to quantity and quality it is not exceeded by any part of America, or perhaps of the world. It is in fact in general use in all private houses, and in the extensive manufactories established through the town. Coal is found in all the hills around this place for ten miles at least, and in such abundance that it may almost be considered the substratum of the whole country. The mines or pits which supply the town, are not further than from one to three miles distant, between the rivers; until within a few years, no coals were brought across the Monongahela, but since the price has been advanced from the increased demand, a considerable supply is now obtained from that quarter. Little short of a million of bushels are consumed annually; the price formerly six cents, has now risen to twelve cents, keeping pace with the increased price of provisions, labour &c. Several of the manufactories have coal pits at their very door, such as those under the Coal hill, which saves the expense of transportation. The coal pits on the side of the Coal hill are about one-third from the top, which is about on a level with the stratum on the opposite side of the river. There are forty or fifty pits opened, including those on both sides of the river. They are worked into the hill horizontally, the coal is wheeled to the mouth of the pit in a wheelbarrow, thrown upon a platform, and from thence loaded into wagons. After digging in some distance, rooms are formed on each side, pillars being left at intervals to support the roof. The coal is in the first instance separated in solid masses, the veins being generally from six to eight feet in thickness, and is afterwards broken into smaller pieces for the purpose, of transportation. A labourer is able to dig upwards of one hundred bushels per day. It is supposed, and perhaps with good reason, that the *main* or principal stratum, lies considerably deeper, as in the English collieries, but the quantity so near the surface of the earth, will for a long period of time render it unnecessary to look for it at a greater depth. Fuel that indispensable necessary of life, is so cheap here, that the poorest rarely suffer from the want of it. We do not witness near Pittsburgh that pitiable spectacle, the feeble infancy and decriped age, of the unfortunate poor, suffering in a cold winter day for a little fire to warm their meagre and chilly blood—we do not see them shivering over a few lighted splinters or pieces of bark, gleaned from the high ways, or torn from the fences, in the skirts of the town.

"As every blessing has its attendant evil, the stone coal is productive of considerable inconvenience from the smoke which overhangs the town, and descends in fine dust which blackens every object; even snow can scarcely be called white in Pittsburgh. The persons and dress of the inhabitants, in the interior of the houses as well as the exterior, experience its effects. The tall steeple of the court house was once painted white, but alas! how changed.

Yet all this might be prevented by some additional expense on the construction of the chimnies. In the English manufacturing towns, a fine is imposed upon those who do not consume their smoke. Incalculable would be the advantage to this place, could such a regulation be adopted. The advantages of cleanliness, and even health, not to mention the improvement in the azure of the sky, and the light of the sun and moon, ought surely to rouse the public spirit of the inhabitants."

The "azure of the sky and the light of the sun and moon" have suffered pretty consistently ever since that coal mine was opened across the river at Coal Hill. They will tell you that the smoke nuisance at Pittsburgh has been abated, that all that talk about soot and grime is just propaganda put out by the Wheeling Commercial Club— but, there's no denying it, there occasionally can be seen a sort of dense dark vaporish mass in the atmosphere in and around Pittsburgh, which if it is not smoke is so similar that it causes strong men to choke and gasp. Yes, there is still some soft-coal smoke around Pittsburgh. In fact, the inhabitants are so conditioned to it that they occasionally suffer shock, convulsions, falling sickness, the bends, and Bang's disease when they leave Allegheny County and venture into the outer atmosphere to Greensburg or Bedford.

The truth is James Kenny reported coal at Redstone Creek early in 1759, and Colonel James Burd, who built the road from Christopher Gist's place to Brownsville, found coal along the Monongahela later in the year. He notes in his journal: "Camp moved two miles to Coal Run. This run is entirely paved in the bottom with fine stone coal . . . I burned about a bushel of this sea coal on my fire." There is a theory among some of the inhabitants of the region today (those who don't own the Encyclopaedia Britannica) that the use of coal for fuel was invented here, the redskins having coached the early settlers in the manner of burning the "black stones." However, we know better than that, it was Wulfred, in A.D. 852, who lined up the first contract.

The outcroppings of coal that these old-timers discovered were part of the Pittsburgh Seam, a fabulous coal deposit extending into four states, covering over 5,700 square miles, and destined to become, on a basis of sale-dollar value, the richest single mineral deposit ever worked in history.

The industrial district for thirty miles around Pittsburgh and the outlying areas beyond are underlaid throughout with bituminous coal of all grades. It is the most important coal area in the United States in size, quality of product, and in variety of coal types. Of the different famous veins, the Pittsburgh Seam yields the most volatile coal, ranging from 33 to 41 per cent in volatile combustion matter. In the Connellsville region, domain of Henry Clay Frick, the "Coke King," we find coal which when roasted in beehive ovens becomes the beautiful pearl-gray Connellsville coke, finest metallurgical fuel in the world. (To the unsuspecting and ignorant train traveler from the flat expanses of the West, the sudden appearance out the train window of row after row of funny-looking beehive ovens glowing in the night is truly startling.) Of the seams occurring in the region, the most important are these: Lower,

Twin, and Upper Freeport; Lower, Middle, and Upper
Kittannings; Pittsburgh and Pittsburgh Big Vein; Sewickley and Piedmont. The output of these mines (which is
omnipresent, whether in barges, gondola cars, coal yards,
trucks, wheelbarrows, piled in back yards, or settling on
the window sill as coal dust) is used in making coke, cement burning, manufacture of illuminating gas, for gen-
erating steam, tile pottery burning, making of producer
gas, and of course for domestic heating purposes.

The manufacture of coke rose to a major industy hand
in hand with the steel industry. After hanging back and arguing his partners down on the idea of going into the steel
business (the firm was already a very big producer of iron,
iron rails, iron bridges, etc.) Andrew Carnegie finally saw
the light and organized a new firm on the banks of the
Monongahela for the manufacture of steel. This mill, the
Edgar Thomson Works, was built on the battlefield where
Edward Braddock was mortally wounded and George
Washington's military coat was shredded with French and
Indian bullets. The mill was started up in 1872 and from
that time on the demand for coke, an ingredient in mak-
ing steel, was constantly increasing.

Chapter 10

Coal by Water

The first coal shipment by water undoubtedly took place when soldiers from the garrison at Fort Pitt rowed or paddled across the Monongahela to Coal Hill, dumped a few bushels from the open outcropping into their craft, and recrossed the river with a cargo of a few hundred pounds for their own use as heating fuel. As the settlement grew, regular pits were opened. As reported in *The Navigator*, there were "forty or fifty pits opened" by 1811. These were commercial diggings, transporting the coal and selling it for profit. Captain Zadok has already told us about the early mining operations, physical equipment, and the miners' output, "upwards of one hundred bushels a day," as well as the fact that manufactories were being built across the river and under Coal Hill, where the fuel to operate them could be mined and tumbled down the hill in chutes right into the boiler room. As more industrial concerns were established, more coal was needed and the natural solution was delivery of coal by boat from mines up the Monongahela; these early coal shipments were on a small scale and handled in open flat boats which were poled down the river. As the reputation of these local coals reached farther and farther down the river, a few coal shipments down the

Ohio were attempted. Thus began a trade that was to last into the twentieth century, and one which at its height was as gaudy a spectacle as the Gold Rush or the Trojan War.

The first coal moving out of the Monongahela to points south was probably carried as ballast in the deep-sea sailing ships which were being built around Pittsburgh at the beginning of the nineteenth century. Shortly thereafter a coal trade per se began, and flats carrying coal cargoes were departing from the Monongahela mines for destinations on the Lower Mississippi.

Once upon a time they sent me down to Cincinnati to bring a towboat up into the Monongahela to the shipyard at Brownsville. The rudders were twisted up like a pretzel and we came up on a flood stage and I had never seen that river before and the boat had no heat on it and, say, it was one swell trip. When we hauled her out on the ways at Brownsville she had a six-inch elm tree stuck in the driving rudder so hard it had to be sawed out. Anyway, speaking of coal coming down out of the Monongahela Valley, it was 2:00 A.M. coming into Pittsburgh and foggy and smoky and I could see a lot of lights every which way, shore lights, bridge lights and all, and nearly got run down by the steamer *Sailor* by getting into a patch of smoke, and here was this dumbbell deckhand up in the pilothouse keeping me company and he says:

"Boss, where do you reckon all the coal comes from anyways?"

"Why, out of the coal mines," I says. "That's about all they got up the Monongahela, just one coal mine after another."

"I mean where did all that there coal come from in the first place? Seems odd now, don't it, all that coal in them mines?"

"Why, man," I said, "that took place a million or more years ago. There was big forests and swamps and the strangest big trees you ever saw. And the trees died and fell into the swamp, they say, and just laid and sludged around in the mud for another million years or so and more trees grew up and kept flopping down on top of them all that time and what with one thing and another they turned into coal and made the coal seams."

"What, a million years ago?"

"Why, sure. That ain't nothing. Maybe fifty million years ago. That's the way it happened and they can prove it too."

"It don't seem likely," he said.

"Don't seem likely to me the world is round," I says. "But that's the way of it. That old coal is just a bunch of trees and plants and stuff."

"Sure don't look like no trees. Looks like coal to me."

"Listen," I says to him, exasperated as hell. "You know what a hog looks like?"

"Yeah. What about it?"

"Well, when you set down to breakfast and cook throws you a couple of slices of bacon, why, it don't resemble hog, would you say?"

"No, but . . ."

"Well, it *is* hog, but it don't look like it," I says. "Now go on down and wash up the dishes. And set a new pot of coffee on the stove while you're at it."

To get back to the coal trade in the early times, as soon as the boys got wind there was money to be made in it, it got to be quite a big operation. The types of craft used for hauling Monongahela coal to western and southern points were merely variations of the flatboats which had been used from earliest times on these waters. They were of deeper draft and generally moved most freely during the high water of the spring and fall seasons. These were one-way barges, that is, they were built to carry cargo downriver, and were broken up at their destination and sold for the scrap lumber; therefore they were made with the minimum structural stability, and were unable to stand any contact, while in motion, with immovable objects, snags, or submerged obstructions. A sharp grounding or severe strain of any kind and the barge simply came apart at the seams and deposited its load on the river bottom and its crew in the river.

In the early days of this trade most of the coal flatboats were built up the Allegheny, more particularly up one of the tributaries called French Creek. As a result of this fact, with the usual imaginative genius of the river fraternity, these boats came to be known as "French creeks." This term, which dates back to the very beginnings of coal towing on the Monongahela, carried over into the golden age of coal towing by steamboats, but in these later times was always specifically used to designate the smaller-sized barges, the large ones being generally lumped together as *coal boats*. These coal boats which were the basic unit of the large tows of the steam towboat era, had dimensions of 160 feet by 24 feet and 6 feet depth.

As they were of box construction, they had an actual capacity of nearly a thousand tons.

As to the coal boats of early times, we have a first hand description of them, as remembered by one Dr. John E. Shaffer, and printed in the Elizabeth, Pa., newspaper in 1887. For the record then:

"The bottoms varied in size. Usually they were about twenty feet wide by one hundred and twenty long, and when loaded drew about five feet of water. The sides of these boats, as well as the ends, were composed of coalboat siding of pine, about one and one-half inches in thickness, and of a width and length corresponding with the size of the timber from which the siding was manufactured. The planks were fastened to the upright stanchions by means of wooden pins made especially for that purpose. When the siding-up was completed the calkers finished the outside by filling the seams with a couple of ropes of oakum which was firmly driven, and when completed made a very close boat.

"There were two boxes constructed on the inner part of each side of every boat, which were to be used as wells, so that in case of the accumulation of water [lovely euphemism for a hell of a leak], by any defect of caulking or from injury to the boat it could be relieved by pumping [by hand! no electric pumps, steam pumps, or gas pumps —just a plain old plunger pump on a spring pole, or maybe not even with the spring pole]. There were check posts, one at each end of the boat. They were logs, set upright, securely fastened to the bottom, extending above the height of the sides. [Today, although made of steel, the

"check posts" on a barge are still called "timberheads."]
They were held in place by strong braces extending out in
every direction, and the coal packed around aided in holding the posts rigid. They were for the tying up of the
boats when landed, immense cables being attached."

So much for the structural features. Pretty primitive
construction. One and a half inch planking, you see, is
nothing at all when a dead weight of coal is to be carried.
No wonder so much coal ended up on the bottom of the
Ohio and the Mississippi.

Above the load, presumably at one end, a rough cabin
was built to furnish shelter for the crew on the long voyage from home. In this crude shanty the provisions were
kept, and the men ate, slept, cussed each other and the
weather, shuffled the greasy pack of cards, passed the jug
of old Monongahely rye, and told great tales of the new
and grand Republic.

These coal boats were sent out in pairs, lashed
together, side by side, with a crew consisting of captain,
relief pilot, cook, and eight or ten wild deckhands, each of
whom was a ferocious bloodthirsty battler, if we believe
the historians. The tonnage of these early two-boat flotil-
las of "French creeks" was from 250 to 750 tons. If the
stage of water was favorable, the trip was made without
incident (other than the gradual reduction in the number
of deckhands due to daily knifings, skull crackings, bone
crushings, eviscerations, eyeball removals, et cetera, as reported by the historians) but if poor water was encoun-
tered, or a run of bad luck came, the maddening difficulties
of a trip could be endless. And in later times, after 1841,

FIGURE 7.   Monongahela pool boat.

the Monongahela locks were a hazard requiring great skill
to negotiate without damage. Then there were the bridges.
Contact of a flimsily built but heavily laden coal boat with
the unyielding and unfriendly bulk of a bridge pier made
a short end to the trip.

The date of the first shipment of coal in barges being
handled by a steamboat is lost, along with the name of the
first deckhand who ever surreptitiously threw a coal scoop
in the river to get out of shoveling coal, and the data on the
first fireman who sent a greenhorn to the engineer for "a
bucket of steam." Some say coal was being shoved around
in barges up the Monongahela in the early 1840's by a
steamboat named *Grampus*. This would seem to be a natural development. No place in the world were there more
steamboats, barges, and coal kicking about than up the
Monongahela. Probably a barge was lashed alongside for
the first experiment. No doubt different combinations of
barges were tried to see what effect they had on the steering. There must have been draft and loading problems.
This was the beginning.

Of historical record we have the first downstream
steamboat-propelled tow leaving Pittsburgh and delivering
three coal boats, or about 10,000 bushels, to Cincinnati in
June, 1845. The steamboat was the *Walter Forward*, which
was owned by a Pittsburgh man named Daniel Bushnell.
Mr. Bushnell had seventeen children and a steamboat.

In 1851 one Hugh Smith purchased the "old side-
wheel packet *Lake Erie* . . . took two coalboats to Cincinnati, lashed alongside, and considering the scheme to have

merit, he made a second trip." The number of his children is not stated.

Also in 1851 Bushnell came back into the picture again, with five more children and a new steamboat, the *Black Diamond*, which he built in partnership with James G. Gray and N. J. Bigley. He had been thinking a lot about facing up to a tow of coal boats instead of carrying them on either side of the towboat, and finally gave orders to Captain Vandergrift to try this system and see how it worked out. He had an idea that maneuverability would be greatly enhanced, and how right he was! Four loads were taken out of the Monongahela to Cincinnati with the steamer shoving from behind, and the system has been used ever since.

The *Crescent City* delivered the first tow of coal to New Orleans from Pittsburgh in 1854. She brought down three coal boats and a barge of coke, 64,000 bushels in all, a very respectable delivery. The downstream trip was made in sixteen days, the up trip in forty. Freight was carried on the return trip also.

All these early towboats were side-wheelers, but by the mid-fifties, stern-wheelers were being used in the coal trade, one of the first being the *W. H. Brown*, built by and named for Captain William H. Brown, who had begun scratching around in the coal game in 1837, and who at his death in '75 was one of the Coal Barons. The stern-wheeler immediately took over the field in the towing business and after the Civil War no more side-wheelers were built for anything but the packet business, car ferries, and so on.

Now in the year of grace 1952, in midstream of the second century of the steamboat age, the curtain is being rung down on the stern-wheel steamer.

Chapter 11

Some Big Tows and Some Big Spills

They say the biggest tow of Monongahela coal ever handled out of the Upper Ohio was the Big Trip made by the *Raymond Horner* in April, 1898. This boat was built at Sewickley in 1881 and was 195 x 45 x 6½ feet, engines 24's with 8-foot stroke and had six western river boilers. She was owned by C. Jutte and Company of Pittsburgh, and Captain Augustus Jutte, one of the best pilots of the time, was up on top for the trip. Although it was customary in the Upper End to run these big tows out in the daylight, Captain Augustus decided to be different and turned loose at 3:00 A.M., picked up the rest of his loads downriver at Safe Harbor, and went on down with 15 loaded coal boats, 3 empty coal boats, 12 barges and the fuel flat, a grand total of 630,000 bushels.

The *Raymond Horner* subsequently was bought by the Combine, got new boilers, had a number of adventures, one of which was having her pilothouse removed with the pilot in it by a low-hanging cable at Dam 18, and was finally sent to the cemetery for the last rites in 1917.

Another record haul out of Pittsburgh was made by the steamer *Tornado*, in the month of May, 1898, when she shoved 16 barges and 6 coal boats from Pittsburgh to Louisville. She was originally built by a famous Negro Captain, G. W. Posey, a licensed steamboat engineer. Her history is rather interesting. She was built complete in only fifty-four days. Her "big spill" was at Cincinnati in 1897, when she sank 17 loaded barges. In 1908, after she had entered the Combine, she went aground one midnight in August on Possum Bar, Clarington, Ohio, with the river falling. She was unable to work off the bar and the river fell, leaving her high and dry, where she remained until the day before Thanksgiving. Finally she was sold to Mexican owners, but after lying at New Orleans for several years until her owners could pluck up the courage to try the deep-water voyage, they started out and she sank off the Mississippi jetties before the trip across the brine had fairly commenced.

Speaking of low water (as above) in September 1881, the marks at Wheeling showed 3 inches below zero. And in August, 1904, the *Ironsides* (of the famous Gray's Iron Line) and the *James Moren* (of the Combine) laid up at Proctor, W.Va., unable to move due to low stage of water until the day after Christmas. Today any towboat with a delay time on her log of *five months* would cause a mass suicide in the home office.

One of the famous coal towboats was the big *Joseph B. Williams*, 211 x 40 x 6½ feet, with condensing engines, 20's, 45's, 9-foot stroke, and six boilers, built in 1876. When practically new she broke her shaft at Island 10 and sprung a

10-foot bend in the hull, but patched up with a *cottonwood tree* she limped back to Pittsburgh. She got her third shaft in 1883, which by 1900 had been in continuous service for seventeen years. Originally owned by the Grand Lake Coal Company, she finally went to the Jutte outfit, who bought this tremendous shover for $21,000, about the value of her galley stove. (She cost $100,000 to build.) In 1898 she faced up to 54 coal boats, 4 barges, and 4 flats, a total of 1,453,000 bushels of coal. She also had some sensational Big Spills. In 1900 she dropped 17 loads out of a tow of 39 at Point Pleasant, Mo. In 1901 she lost 10 loads. In 1903 she lost 23 coal boats out of a tow of 31, down below Natchez.

The *W. W. O'Neil*, one of the big girls in the coal fleets made a famous trip in 1907 with 28 coal boats and 2 model barges of steel from Louisville to New Orleans in 9 days 14 hours, landing but once, to clean boilers, and running the Cairo and Memphis bridges at night with no assistance from tugs, a feat which causes this deckhand's hair to stand on end. In July, 1900, she was bound up with 22 empties, quite a good upstream tow; she usually took 14 or 15 on the uptrip. This boat was noted among rivermen for her unholy consumption of fuel coal. She was the only towboat besides the *Sprague* to have a 12-foot stroke. Cylinders 26″ diameter. Died in 1913 after thirty-two years of noble service.

The *Tom Dodsworth* (no relation to Sam), built in Pittsburgh in 1871, once took nine loads from Pittsburgh to Cincinnati and returned with two empties in 4 days 20 hours 15 minutes. In 1900 she hit the tow of the *Volun-*

teer at Swan Creek sinking *twenty* of the *Volunteer's* barges and four of her own. In 1902 at the ripe old age of thirty-one she stood a "good inspection" for U.S. Steamboat Inspectors Maddy and Morgan at Middleport. Hung on until 1917 and wasn't dismantled until 1925, aged fifty-four years.

The *Boaz*, a famous old-timer who towed coal out of the Monongahela to points south for many years, had some beautiful mishaps. Ran aground on a falling river on the Lower Mississippi in 1901 with a 42-piece tow, and remained high and dry. Had a glorious spill in 1895, sinking her entire tow of 14 loads above Hawesville. On another occasion the boat was headed down with 32 loads when all of a sudden the fog shut down without warning (it'll do that) in a mighty bad piece of river near Ashland, Ky.; the tow hit a bridge pier and it was good-bye to 12 coal boats. Captain Frank Gould was winding the big wheel on the *Boaz* that night, and George Parshall was mate. The pilot wheel of the *Boaz* is one of the largest in existence; it has been preserved and was exhibited at the River Exposition in Pittsburgh in 1938. Captain Fred Way, Jr., says there is a legend that the *Boaz* "left Pittsburgh on a rise with a large tow of coal, commenced 'dropping' barges in minor accidents here and there, and before she got to Cincinnati had lost them all, and had to return to Pittsburgh for more." They should have had radar. *Boaz*, R.I.P., 1916.

In January, 1911, four Pittsburgh towboats were downbound with steel and Monongahela coal as follows:

Sprague, 52 pieces; *Boaz,* 36; *Oakland,* 36; *Harry Brown,* 30. Just a typical group of tows.

In December, 1899, the Monongahela River Consolidated Coal and Coke Company (the "Combine") shipped 876 barges and 512 coal boats south with 24,552,000 bushels of coal.

The big steamer *Oakland* lost ten loads going down in 1911, two at Louisville, two at Uniontown, Ky., and climaxed the trip by hitting the bank at Round Lake, sinking six more.

In December, 1897, the *Sam Brown,* owned by the W. H. Brown Sons, one of the earliest big coal operators, ran ashore at Fish Creek and dumped nine coal boats and two barges, and damaged the boat to the tune of a $3,000 repair bill. Not much profit on that trip.

These coal towboats sometimes waited for weeks or months for a suitable stage of water. In January, 1904, the *Gleaner* had been waiting for a rise at Louisville for six months. Easy work for the pilots but tough on the company. In June, 1903, the Combine had 32 towboats hitched up to their tows waiting to go south if and when the river co-operated with a rise.

Here's some good low-water work: in December, 1901, the *J. B. Finley,* big Combine towboat, shoved 36 empties upstream from Cincinnati to Littleport on a stage of 4½ feet. One of the pilots was Captain Henry Nye, a famous stargazer of the days of the big tows.

In 1902 the *Fred Wilson* sank eight coal boats on Twelve Pole Bar. Owned by coal operators W. W. O'Neil

& Company, she blew up below the canal at Louisville in 1904 and was a total loss. Captain Joe Price, among others, was killed in the explosion.

At the same time in 1902 the *Sam Brown* lost four barges and the *Hornet* sank three and the fuel flat.

Nowadays a single sunken barge is a comparatively rare occurrence and an incident of considerable embarrassment to the pilot and mate on watch. One of the most mystifying barge losses in modern times happened to a Federal Barge Line boat on the Lower Mississippi; a barge in the tow sank in the night and was not missed until the watch changed. The barge was never found. I have this from a deckhand who claims to have been aboard at the time. This story is not patented or copyrighted for translation into foreign tongues. It was told to me on good authority but is possibly a lie. There, now I'm covered on that one. And speaking of barge losses, one of the swellest in history happened in Minneapolis in April, 1951, when a barge broke loose and was carried down onto the Ford Dam. When the damages on this seemingly trivial, though exciting, incident were added up they came to $828,200 as follows: $750,000 damage to the dam, $41,200 damage to the barge, $12,000 loss and damage to the cargo, and $25,000 damage to the Milwaukee bridge which the barge slammed into on the way down to the dam. When last heard from, the Central Barge Company, owners of the barge, were suing the city of Minneapolis for the full amount on eighteen counts of negligence. (The docks are city operated.) This shows what happens when a runaway barge gets real mad.

In March, 1905, the Combine sank five coal boats of 25,000 bushels each, plus a barge containing 12,000 kegs of nails (presumably from Wheeling) at Merrimans.

In March, 1905, while the titanic *Sprague* was pushing 1,200,000 bushels of coal down the Ohio, the Combine towboat *Valiant* socked the bridge pier at Kenova and sank a few barges of coal. Anybody in the audience want to ask any questions?

And now they're all gone, all the Combine boats and all the coal boats, and the farm kids along the Ohio never run down to the riverbank any more to see those acres and acres of black Monongahela coal sliding slowly downstream, driving the chutes and flanking the bends, hanging up on bars, slamming the bridge piers, and causing consternation, excitement, and joy throughout the beautiful valley.

Finally, to give you the full flavor of the old coal-towing days, I am going to include here the obituary notice from the *Waterways Journal* of "the dean of the old-time coal boat pilots," Captain Henry B. Nye. The article is accompanied by a picture of Captain Nye. He looks like a Roman senator, with a majestic brow and regal features, and a pair of the clearest eyes that ever looked out of the pages of our beloved "riverman's bible."

"All the darkies down on the riverfront are aweeping. The last cast of 'no bottom' on the lead line has been relayed to the pilot house. The lead whistle has blown the lead heavers off. The last shoal crossing has been made, and a voice cries out in the far off dim distance of another world. ' "Poor Boy" is dead.'

"Capt. Henry B. Nye, the dean of all oldtime coal boat pilots, has changed watches for the last time. Henry Buckingham Nye was born at Pomeroy, Ohio, August 28, 1858. His father Buckingham Coster Nye, who was known amongst the river fraternity as 'Buck' Nye, was himself a pioneer of the river game. He was an engineer of rare ability. Thus his son, by this environment, was endowed to devote his life to the profession of piloting boats.

"In his early twenties, Henry Nye started out on a long career of usefulness and ability that may be equalled but never excelled. For more than 50 years, whenever boating was mentioned or discussed, Henry Nye's name became a symbol of efficiency and ability. From Pittsburgh, Pa., 'On the Beautiful Ohio,' with her blazing furnaces and steel mills, to New Orleans, La., on the muddy waters of the Mississippi, with her balmy Gulf breezes, Henry Nye's name has been carved in the memory of rivermen.

"The writer likes to recall some of the interesting stories this Grand Old Man narrated to him several years ago. His first job as a pilot after he received his license, was towing stone out of Apple Creek, below Grand Tower, Ill. How vividly he remembered standing on the river bank at Mound City, Ill., in the early sixties, and watching General Grant pass by with the gun boats that later captured Fort Donaldson and Fort Henry.

"After several years of river work, having established himself as a successful pilot, he accepted a job with the Combine piloting the large coal tows from Louisville, Ky., to New Orleans, La., on such boats as the *Joseph B. Williams, Finley, Harry Brown, Alice Brown, exporter, W. W.*

O'Neil and many others. Then when the *Sprague*, one of the largest towboats on inland rivers was completed and placed in service, Capt. Nye and Capt. Calvin Blazier, (often affectionately called 'Poor Boy' and 'Quaker Oats,' respectively, by rivermen) became her pilots. It was then that one of the largest coal tows ever made came down the river. We find Capt. Henry Nye at the wheel. The tow consisted of 60 coal boats, the dimensions of which were 180 feet long, 26 feet beam and eight feet draft. The tow was arranged five lengths, 12 barges wide. The tonnage was 50,000. People lined the river banks to see the mighty tow of 'Black Diamond' pass by. For 14 years Capt. Nye was pilot on the *Sprague*.

"In 1915 Capt. Nye became an employe of the West Kentucky Coal Company of Paducah, Ky., where he remained until he retired in 1934 . . .

"After leaving the river Capt. Nye resided with Mr. and Mrs. Al Harrigan in their palatial home on Kentucky Avenue, Paducah. In this home he fixed up an office, and in it one would find log books covering the data of river laws, river gauges, channel changes and a complete record of his more than 50 years spent at a pilot wheel. He never became weary of trying to give any youngster helpful advice sought that might be beneficial to him as a pilot. Today as one leaves the Ohio River and enters the Mississippi River on the Kentucky shore, he finds a light named 'Quaker Oats' in memory of Capt. Calvin Blazier, and only a few miles below, one on the Missouri shore named Henry Nye. Nothing could be more fitting and proper, as these two names should always be associated together.

FIGURE 8. IRON WORKS ON THE MONONGAHELA NEAR PITTSBURGH, 1896.

"A new day has dawned in river heaven as Henry Nye has joined hands with Capts. Calvin Blazier, John Pierce, James Martin, Clarence Carter, William Smith, Walter Carroll, Ed Pell and Bill Crowe. Everyone is posting up, and I imagine I can hear Capt. Blazier ask Henry, 'How do you run Plum Point?' Or Johnny Pierce ask about Old Town Bend. Or Clarence Carter say, 'Henry, can you steer Craighead Point with four lengths?' Or 'Dude' Pell ask about the set on Cairo Bridge. Or Jimmy Martin ask, 'What do you think of the cutoffs?' Then someone asks, 'What about Capt. Harvey Brown, Capt. Graham Varble, Capt. Elmer Good, Capt. Gene Hampton, Capt. John Hottell, Capt. Bill Edwards, Capt. Henry Lindenburn, Capt. Pete Briscoe, Capt. Charley Nadal?' And Capt. Henry replies, 'Boys, they are still dropping the big tows down in the bends.'

"Henry Nye has visited them all and everybody is well posted. And whatever may come or go, Capt. Nye's name will become a monument of integrity, wisdom and ability upon which the river world will gaze with eyes of admiration forever and ever."

Chapter 12

"*Unspeakable Old Monongahela*"

"That drove the spigot out of him!" cries Stubb. " 'Tis July's immortal Fourth; all fountains must run wine to-day! Would now it were old Orleans whisky, or old Ohio, or unspeakable old Monongahela!"
—*Moby Dick; or The White Whale*

Bernard De Voto said it like this:

"Whiskey has been the drink of patriots ever since freedom from her mountain-height unfurled her banner to the air. The American people achieved nationality and Old Monongahely in the same generation, which should surprise no one, since nations flower swiftly once their genius has budded. Take the Irish. They were a breed of half-naked cave dwellers sunk in ignorance and sin and somewhat given to contentiousness. Then the gentle St. Patrick appeared among them. He taught them to make usquebaugh and at once they became the most cultured people in the world.

"Or take the Indians. They were a genial people on whom we inflicted repulsive cruelties. (For instance, after

133

the French had educated them to brandy we corrupted their taste with rum.) Yet a philosopher may wonder whether they had it in them to rise to cultural distinction. They evoke both pity and dismay: north of Mexico they never learned to make a fermented beverage, still less a distilled one. That they had ingenuity is not to be denied and one of their achievements is a marvel: They took a couple of wild grasses and bred them up to corn. But what did they do with corn? Century succeeded century and, content to regard it as a mere food, they could not meet the challenge on which, as Mr. Toynbee recognizes, civilization hung. Every damp spell rotted some of their stored corn. The historian watches, his breathing suspended, and sees the pointer settle toward decline. They threw the stuff out for the birds, rebuking their supernaturals, and never knew that the supernaturals had given them a mash.

"The Americans got no help from heaven or the saints but they knew what to do with corn. In the heroic age our forefathers invented self-government, the Constitution, and bourbon, and on the way to them they invented rye. ('If I don't get rye whiskey I surely will die' expresses one of Mr. Toynbee's inexorable laws of history more succinctly than ever he did.) And that shows our proper place in the international order: no other nation ever gave mankind two whiskeys. Like our political institutions, which would be inconceivable without them, both express our national characteristics; both are distilled not only from our native grains but from our native vigor, suavity, generosity, peacefulness, and love of accord."

After that beautiful calliope music, anything I or anyone else might have to say is likely to be an anticlimax.

I was sitting around in the bar of the Hotel Mark Twain in St. Louis one rainy Tuesday with a bunch of steamboat pilots, high- and low-pressure engineers, active and inactive deckhands, mates, and students of sandbar and willow tree on the Upper Mississippi, Missouri, Gasconade, Big Sandy, Wisconsin, St. Croix, Kanawha, Cumberland, Black, Zumbro, Galena, and other rivers, including one pioneer from the Hennepin Canal and another veteran who claimed to have steamboated with "Old Rough-Head" Heckman, when I got somebody's highball by mistake.

"Something has gone wrong here," I said. "The boy has given me a drink that tastes like up around the Calumet-Sag someplace."

"I imagine you got my drink by mistake," said one of the group.

"You're very welcome to have it back," I said, "for I am not enjoying the flavor, but tell me, friend, where do you come from and just exactly what is that beverage?"

"That, captain, is—"

"I am unemployed at present," I said.

"That is the finest nectar in the civilized world—in short it is Monongahela rye whisky."

"Well, that's all very interesting," I said, "but if it's all the same to you I b'lieve I will stick to this fluid from Peoria on the Illinois."

"Perfectly O.K. with me," he replied.

"Sure, I was deckhand on the *Dan Converse*," said an ancient mariner to no one in particular. "We run to

Fort Benton in four days and ten hours one time from the St. Louis levee."

"Fast trip," says one. "About forty miles an hour. Pretty good for a steamboat."

"Well, Ben," said another, "she was snagged and a total loss up above St. Joe on the Missouri in 1858. That makes you a hundred years old, providing you was decking when you was eight years old."

"You must be wrong about that date," says the first aged salt, who was approaching his fifty-first birthday. "I'll have another beer."

"Yes," says the second, gazing lovingly into his glass of rye, "and the *Dan Converse* was built just a few miles from my home, down at McKeesport on the old Mon, in 1855. A stern-wheeler—163 tons, I believe."

"I suppose you was at the launching, Irvin," says a Pittsburgh pools man who had just strolled up.

"And we christened her with a full quart of Monongahela rye whisky," said Irvin. "Those were glorious times on the Mon, why, they were dumping as many as forty, fifty steamboats a year in the river from our shipyards."

"I suppose you was pretty good buddies with old Captain Henry Shreve, too, wasn't you?" says a skeptic in the crowd from the Galena River. "He didn't die until around 1845."

"No, he was before my time," says Irvin. "I was just a kid in '55."

That was the first time I ever tasted rye whisky. Little did I know how the first trans-Allegheny pioneers depended on this liquid to keep up their morale. Why, when you delve into the matter and consult the authorities on the subject, it looks like those early settlers out there spent more time passing the bottle than they did at shooting Mingos. And it appears that this frontier practice included the Baptists, Methodists, Zinzendorfian Brethren, Old German Reformeds, Covenanters, Seceders, Associate Reformeds, the Campbellites, the New Lights, the Free Will Baptists, and all the other religious species in the area, not just the irresponsible and unbaptized.

Now listen to what one Van Voorhis, a Monongahela historian, has to say on the matter: "The use of spirits as a beverage in olden time was a prevailing custom. Late as sixty years ago [1830] it was considered a breach of etiquette not to set out the bottle when friends and even ministers called on a visit. The green-glass, long-necked quart bottle was a kind of a household god. It was present on nearly every occasion. At weddings, corn-huskings, wood-choppings, log-rollings, flax-pullings, manure frolics, sheep-washing, fish gigging, house and barn raisings, it was an essential element."

What is this "manure frolics"? I've been to some rough parties down around Scotts Run but don't think I ever recall anything exactly answering this description.

Back in those days almost everybody made his own hooch, as it was the most profitable thing to do with the rye crop. It took twenty days for a pack horse to make the trip over the mountains from Pittsburgh to Philadelphia, and the average horse could carry only 4 bushels of rye. But the horse could carry 24 bushels of rye once it had been converted in the old home still, or the community still, into 8 gallons of rye whisky. And with the high rates for transport this was not a small matter.

These early Monongahela Valley farmers were mostly Scotch-Irish and had learned all the fine points of manufacturing grain spirits back in their homeland, where they were handed down from generation unto generation to the greater glory of mankind. They knew how to make fine whisky and they drank a considerable portion of what they made. There was a ready and profitable market for the surplus, and there you are. In the 1790's there were about 1,300 stills operating in western Pennsylvania, which is a hell of a lot of stills. In fact in this small area were 25 per cent of all the stills in the new United States. This figure does not include many small stills which were operated for family consumption. Every crossroads had its distillery where thirty, forty, or fifty farmers brought their rye, just as to a gristmill.

The earliest distillery we know of in Pittsburgh was founded in 1769 by Jonathan Plumber. When George Washington visited in 1770 he sampled the product and declared it was "excellent whisky." The output of this and other early distilleries was not only used to slake the local thirst, but was a vital ingredient in the fur trade. A letter about 1785 from "the Salt Works" to Craig & Bayard, Pittsburgh distillers, says: "I am greatly in want of three barrels of whisky and a barrel of rum. For want of them, my neighbor gets all the skins and furs."

As the old mariner himself, Zadok Cramer, says in discussing the Monongahela, "The best and greatest quantity of rye whisky is made on this river. Peach and apple brandy, cider and cider-royal are also made in great abundance." And he says that in 1807 there were two distilleries in Pittsburgh alone making 1,200 barrels of whisky per year.

That the conversion of grain to whisky was more profitable than milling grain, and far more profitable than conversion of grain to livestock, appears to be indicated by a list of prices in the Pittsburgh *Gazette* for April, 1794:

> WHISKY—22 shillings, 6 pence per gallon
> FLOUR—25 shillings per barrel
> MUTTON—3 pence per lb. wholesale
> MUTTON—4 pence per lb. retail

The year 1794 must have been an inflation period because another high-proof authority on the subject says that in pioneer days of the Pennsylvania and West Virginia frontier, whisky was at times used as the chief medium of exchange, and that "a gallon of prime rye whisky was equivalent to a shilling." Two barrels of whisky would buy "a good corner lot in a growing village."

Later on, Monongahela rye whisky played an important part in the construction of the early railroads, as it appears to have been one of the leading items of diet for the Irish laborers on the work gangs. During the boring of the tunnel at Griegsville, "scarcely a day passed without the sight of a number of wagons loaded with flour, bacon, and whisky leaving the stores of the town [Morgantown] for the line of construction." On one occasion a runaway horse caused the immediate and total destruction of a wagonload of seven choice barrels of Monongahela whisky en route to the railroad. However, enough of the genuine goods reached the construction crews to contribute effectively to the "numerous riots and brawls between the opposing factions of Corkonians and Fardowns who severely tried the physical ability of the sheriff's *posse comitatus.*" In fact, in July, 1851, a hundred well-loaded representatives from Ireland staged a battle which began at the east end of the tunnel, raged throughout the night, ended up at daybreak at the west end. Shillelaghs, stones, and pistols were the weapons used, and to such stimulating effect that "four or five" persons were killed. The editor of the Morgantown *Mirror* comments that but for Irish awkwardness in the use of firearms a much larger number of coffins would have been required. On another occasion, following the arrival of a shipment of rye whisky at the railroad camp at Fairmont, a gigantic shillelagh party took place resulting in the arrest of so many Irish empire builders that the jail went down to her overload marks and two hacks full of rye whisky enthusiasts had to be taken over the mountains to the jail at Morgantown. And it was to the merry sound of such celebrations as these that the "end of track" pushed ever westward. Thus Monongahela rye contributed to the building of the young nation.

Still later, in Civil War times, Morgantown was occupied by rebels in a raid in April, 1863. During the occupation, which was a pretty tame affair punctuated by a considerable amount of giggling conversation between the young ladies and the boys in gray, the general put guards over the saloons and the drugstores to keep the boys from temptation. However, the general departed finally, leaving about two hundred men behind, who, being as thirsty as any Corkonian or Fardown, promptly got into the whisky. One private by the name of Bushrod Washington, being "about half seas over," apologized to the ladies for drinking so much, but excused himself on the grounds that the whisky here in the Monongahela country was so much better than what they got in the Confederacy that he could not restrain himself.

I have been trying to find some concrete facts about the actual operations of a typical Monongahela distillery. A Philadelphian (who says he is partial to a brand of liquid ecstasy known as "Conestoga Rye") gives a description of one of the biggest, John Gibson's Son & Company. This was written about 1870, in one of those volumes bragging up the local industries. It doesn't tell how whisky is made but it does tell of the scale of operations once the thing got organized on a commercial basis. From the farm-owned copper still to the giant distillery with important brick smokestacks and bookkeepers in green eyeshades was a natural development that took place alongside of the rise of the steamboat, and the growth of the coal and iron industries.

"The late John Gibson commenced the liquor business about the year 1840, and, in 1856, erected the Gibsonton Mills Distillery on the Monongahela River. This distillery is considered the finest establishment of the kind in the country, and its products have long enjoyed a very wide celebrity . . . They have at the present time actually invested in the trade a heavy capital, estimated at $3,500,000. Their capacity of production is 150 barrels

per diem of fine whisky, which—valued at $80 per barrel
—represents a daily product of $12,000. This whisky is
manufactured only from the best quality of rye grown in
Pennsylvania and West Virginia. The stock usually carried by the firm is about 25,000 barrels of different ages,
valued in round figures at $3,000,000. The amount of
taxes paid by the house into the United States Treasury
amounts to over $2000 every day, being $750,000 yearly.
They give employment to 200 hands . . . The great
establishment at 232 and 234 South Front Street, Philadelphia, is sufficiently important to deserve more than a
passing notice. The main business of this house is the grad-
ing of fine whiskies, in which department the firm trans-
acts a very large trade. Whiskies of different ages are
brought from the distillery when fit for use, and blended
together after the method usually employed in the grad-
ing or blending of French brandies. On the second and
third floors are 400 staved casks, capable of containing
about 320 gallons each, in which the whiskies are retained
until perfectly bright and fit for shipping. At this establishment the firm daily manufacture 150 barrels of French
spirit, rectified whisky, gin, and domestic brandy . . .
The Gibsonton works are under the supervision of the
firm in Philadelphia, and it is not too much to say, that
the routine of the business in all its details is attended to
with a precision not surpassed in any military camp in the
world. The other buildings are two large bonded warehouses—one being 110 by 50 feet, and the other 93 by 50
feet—having an aggregate capacity of 9000 barrels. These
two rooms are detached from those already described, and

are provided with doors and shutters made of strong boiler iron. The walls are of solid stone 2½ to 3 feet thick, and four stories high, with basements; the roofs are of slate with brick cornices. All the warehouses are constructed with a view to support the enormous weight which each floor is destined to carry . . . The system of heating the rooms is by steam, and is perfect in principle and detail . . . No artificial lights are used in these buildings under any pretext. The heat is kept at a uniform temperature of 80 degrees, both in winter and summer, and by this means the whisky is brought to the requisite maturity to suit it for the market. In addition to these structures, there are cooper shops, where the firm manufacture all the barrels used in the establishment."

So there was whisky. There was whisky in the valley of the Monongahela and there was fine rye whisky in the bars of the Ohio River packets and in the St. Louis hotels. Jugs of Old Monongahely were passed around out on the Republican and the Belle Fourche and the Niobrara. Westmoreland County rye was available at Galena, at Red Wing, at Leadville, at Independence, out in the sagebrush and up in the mountains. The men wore beards, chewed tobacco, and drank barrels of whisky. It was quite a country then, before the invention of the juke box and the rum coke.

This reminds me of an old boy down around Beardstown on the Illinois who went out in his skiff one afternoon in November with the old twelve-gauge to blast out a few ducks. The ducks were flying when he left his houseboat but they had all gone off someplace else once he got out in the sloughs. So he kept plugging away at this old quart of rye he had along with him. Next day they found him in the skiff on his back frozen into three inches of solid bilge ice. Took him to the hospital and put a blow-torch on him and thawed him out.

The following Saturday he got his limit.

Chapter 13

"*I Walked into the Mine*"

"I was born one mornin' when the sun didn't shine,
I picked up my shovel and walked into the mine,
Loaded sixteen tons of the number nine coal . . ."
—Merle Travis

I'm not a coal miner, never was one, but I lived in the coal country, inhaled the coal atmosphere, quaffed many a foaming beaker of Tube City or Iron City or Duquesne brew with the coal miners, listened to their tales, worked with their sons on the coal towboats, and even made love to their daughters.

In the first coal mines the digging was done by picks, the power supplied by arms and shoulders, and the coal hauled to the mine entrance in small wagons. In a particularly gloomy early volume on the subject, there is a picture showing the use of women as beasts of burden in hauling coal out of the very early English coal mines. I feel sure that no Sallys, Phoebes, or Janes were called up in the Monongahela diggings to haul coal trucks, but dogs, man's second best friend, were extensively used for this purpose.

The demand for coal was great and, as we have seen, eventually coal became an item for export far beyond the immediate area. Hence mines multiplied, particularly those of the Pittsburgh Seam (which is the vein opening in the hills bordering the Monongahela, and which has been worked continuously from the very beginning) until it was impossible to go up the river to Brownsville from Pittsburgh without being contantly in sight of mines, mine tipples, and loading docks. There are something like 150 mines in the 55 miles above Lock 1.

Since the Pittsburgh Seam rises and falls in synclines and anticlines over the area, the mines are at different levels, sometimes, as at Elizabeth, being very low, permitting tipples to be operated directly at the mouth of the mine, and at other times high in the steep and rugged hills. The typical nineteenth-century coal mine was dug into the hillside facing the river. Conventional mule and narrow-gauge trucks had come in to take the place of buckets, baskets, or dog-and-wagon transport from the interior of the mine. A car, reaching the mouth of the mine, was switched onto an inclined track down to the tipple below. A cable was made fast to it, which ran over a drum, and the weight of the descending loaded car pulled up, on the opposite track, the empty which had preceded it and was at the bottom. Arriving at the tipple, the loaded coal car dumped into an inclined chute, where by means of various screens the coal was sorted into lump, nut, dust, etc., and thence dropped into the barge tied up under the tipple chute in the river.

As I understand it, digging coal in the old days was a

job requiring a real man and went like this: First a cut was made under the coal at floor level; this was called "bearing in." It was done with a hand pick, lying on one's side on a rough and lumpy surface in a dark and smelly hole in the ground. After this undercutting was done the coal face was sheared down along the two sides, also done with a hand pick (and the air not getting any better). Finally, the block of coal thus outlined was knocked down, by means of iron wedges driven in at the top of the block. Obviously it quite often happened that the coal fell on the miner, in which case he was usually damaged, frequently requiring the services of a preacher.

At other times miners were caught under masses of slate falling from the roof, under cave-ins caused by collapse of improper timber supports, and of course by explosions due to mine gas. There was no inspection, little attention was paid to anything like a safety program, and the fatalities were high.

It was in such manner that the production of coal was carried on for many many years in the Monongahela basin, as well as in all the other coal fields of the country. Scores of companies were engaged in mining coal, shipping coal, peddling coal, toasting coal into coke, and otherwise showing the old American pep. Presumably they were already thinking up sales slogans and running off contests between the salesmen, the prize being a new briefcase and a ton of coal, or a horseshoe stickpin.

Some of the individuals engaged in this black and dusty enterprise made great fortunes, built large and hideous castles with frightening stained-glass windows, and otherwise made themselves objects of regard and envy. One such famous Coal Baron was William H. Brown, who began in a small way peddling coal from door to door in Pittsburgh. Born in Westmoreland County, Pennsylvania, in 1815, he worked on farms and on the canalboats, and then became a coal miner. He bought a horse and wagon and began to make his own deliveries. Then he became part owner of a mine. He withdrew from this partnership because his associates could not see any future either in making coke or in marketing surplus coal down the river. A new firm was formed—Lloyd, Black & Brown,—and it quickly became a big success. Brown designed an improved coal boat, stronger than the old type, but lighter than the barge of the time, and in a fleet of these, great shipments were made to New Orleans, St. Louis, and points between. Brown made a killing, too, during the Civil War, supplying the armies and the gunboat fleets. In 1875 the former canalboat deckhand died leaving a six million dollar estate.

The Pittsburgh Seam was estimated after the Civil War to contain 54 billion tons of coal, and it was appraised as being of greater value than the total output of the California gold mines for one thousand years. Seven thousand men were employed in the mines in 1868, producing 2½ million tons of coal annually, of which two-thirds was barged out of the Monongahela and down the Ohio. Even as early as this there were 120 steamboats working on coal shipments, 40 of them used downstream, the rest in the pools of the Monongahela and around the mines, in harbor work, and other local jobs.

By 1885 half a million tons of coal were moving out of the Monongahela to New Orleans, and another quarter million tons to various sugar producers in the South. The improvement of the channel at the mouth of the Mississippi in 1890 made New Orleans a coaling station for ocean-going vessels, further increasing the demand and resulting in Monongahela Valley clinkers and ash being dumped in such far places as the North Sea and the Indian Ocean.

On the Monongahela itself there has never been a real slump in river tonnage since the very early beginnings. The Ohio River lost a great deal of its coal freight, and its packet business went through many periods of boom and bust, ending in a conclusive bust; but the steamboat whistles kept on warbling up and down the Monongahela right on through the years. Meanwhile many of the Ohio tributaries, formerly carrying heavy tonnage, have ceased to exist as commercial waterways. The Upper Mississippi also fell on hard times—first the packets were driven out by the railroads, and then, after the lumbering interest had cleaned out Wisconsin and Minnesota, the rafting business came to a dead stop and the river was virtually deserted until the slack-water system of locks and dams was put in. Galena, Ill., once the largest port on the Upper Mississippi where eight or ten magnificent steamboats often tied up at one time, is silted in now, and the Fever River will barely float a homemade skiff. The citizens haven't heard a steamboat whistle since 1914 and will never hear this sentimental music again. The Upper Missouri is a dead duck as far as steamboating is concerned; a steamboat could no more get to Fort Benton, Mont. today than it could take a coal tow to Spitsbergen. The same ups and downs, boom and bust (mostly bust), took place on the Minnesota, the Kentucky, the Hocking, the Licking, the Scioto, the White, the Chippewa, the Green, the Big Sandy, the Muskingum, the Wisconsin, and the Wabash. Up in Alaska at St. Michaels the bones of the *Portus B. Weare*, the *John J. Healy*, and the others who made Yukon history, lie in the graveyard of steamboats. Far up the Allegheny all is still, no boats where once were many. The Des Moines River is dead. No more packets up the West Fork above Fairmont. The Maquoketa is bankrupt. But in one week in January, 1951, Lock 2 on the Mononga-hela had the biggest tonnage in its history; and it has had a steadily increasing traffic ever since the first Indian on the banks shoved his canoe into the stream.

But since this chapter was supposed to be about coal mines, here's the story of the big blowup at Monongah, up at the headwaters of the Monongahela on the West Fork River across the bridge from Fairmont. This explosion, which took place on December 6, 1907, enjoys the lugubrious distinction of being the worst mine disaster in history: Three hundred and sixty-one miners died in a series of explosions and fires which completely wrecked two large mines. It was six weeks, during which time rescue crews from West Virginia, Pennsylvania, Maryland, and Ohio toiled around the clock, before the last of the bodies was brought out of the mine. Practically the entire town of 6,000 was in mourning, hardly a family without a loss. *Not a single man in the mines at the time of the explosion lived.* Only four ever came out alive; they managed to crawl out through a ventilation shaft, but all died a few days later of injuries and exposure.

A great "tide of public indignation" spread as a result of this grisly and horrifying affair. Investigating committees were immediately formed to study the causes of the disaster, and to devise safety measures to prevent such another event. As a direct result, the federal government created the Federal Bureau of Mines, to set up and enforce safety regulations in U.S. mines, since which time the hazards of the industry have been greatly reduced.

It is still no picnic, however, and it still takes a man to be a coal miner.

Once upon a time we had a big redheaded boy from Booth, W.Va., riding as deckhand and he was about half useless. He didn't like it on the river and he was all the time complaining about the hours and the wages and the food and he was tiresome as hell but still he stayed.

"How come you ride this old towboat then, if you don't like it?" I asked him one evening, coming down into Round Bottom.

"Ain't nothing else *to* do," he said. "My old man he tole me ifn I went to work in the mine he'd skin me alive. If you knew my old man you'd know he meant it, too."

"Why, say, your old man's a miner himself, ain't he?"

"I reckon he is. He been in the mine for thirty-five years. That's jest the point. Me and my brothers he says he'll split our skulls wide open with a shovel if we so much as go into the mine. He'd do it too, by God."

Chapter 14

The Combine

The rise of long-distance coal towing out of the Monongahela to southern markets, which had begun way back in the eighteenth century, culminated in a colossal operation with the fine title of "The Monongahela River Consolidated Coal and Coke Company," known as the Combine. Formed in 1899 with a capital of $40,000,000, it was to the other barge lines what Everest is to Coal Hill, across the river from Pittsburgh. Competition had become very tough after W. H. Brown died in '75. Newly developed coal regions of the Kanawha River began to cut in on the game, Alabama coal also was getting a lot of the business, and other states nearer the South were supplying more and more of the coal formerly coming from the Monongahela. The Monongahela shippers were cutting each other's throats and getting nowhere.

Pittsburgh having been the stage for the Carnegie mergers as well as the scene of many other financial and industrial feats of magic and mystification, it was perfectly natural that to face the new conditions in the southern coal-towing business the idea of a merger or combine would be forthcoming. And so it was that almost all of the independent coal producers and shippers engaged in Monongahela operations decided to surrender their holdings when some high-powered operators got together and promoted the idea of the Combine. They sold out everything, their total line of equipment and goodwill, including all their towboats, barges, coal boats, mines, tipples, coal landings, docks, marine ways, and other assets on the banks of the Monongahela, as well as coalyards, docks, landings, sidings, etc., on the Ohio and Mississippi. Some of the coal operators also took stock in the new colossus, some sold out for cash and turned to other enterprises. There were plenty of customers for a fast promotion around Pittsburgh and the stock was similar to hot cakes in sales appeal and was greatly oversubscribed. In addition to finding itself in possession of extensive holdings in active mines and coal-rich land, the new organization now owned about *eighty* towboats and tugs, plus thousands of barges, coal boats, hulks, and flats for bulk shipment of Monongahela River coal and coke.

One of the men in on the deal was Henry Oliver, an exceedingly active and animated person with his thumb and fingers as well as his feet in a hundred schemes, combinations, and promotions all the time. Frequently his enthusiasm and energy were misdirected and he would go bust with a glorious display of fireworks, only to pick himself up, get a shave, and make another fortune before suppertime. He was one of the "bottom Hoosiers" with whom the Carnegie boys played as children in the Rebecca Street days before they began to play with corporations and mountain ranges, and he had also been a fellow

messenger boy with Carnegie in the Pittsburgh telegraph office. When he heard about the discovery of iron
ore in the Mesabi Range in Minnesota he rushed to Du-
luth, found the joint hopping with prospectors, had to
sleep on the billiard table at the hotel, finally found Leo-
nidas Merritt, the discoverer of the range, made pals with
him, slipped him some good checks on Pittsburgh and
New York banks, and became the owner of many many
acres of that peculiar powdery ore. Subsequently he made
millions on it. To a man like this, always as excited as a
kid on Christmas Eve at the prospect of a new venture,
the idea of a giant coalition of mines, steamboats, and
barges was duck soup.

The Combine prospered. By improving methods in
mining, handling, and marketing their coal they were able
to cut costs and build up their sales. Huge quantities of
coal now left the Monongahela again for points on the
Ohio, the Lower Mississippi, and the Middle Mississippi
as far up as St. Louis, where they had a contract for coal
with the Laclede Gas Company. In the first month of operation, that of December, 1899, the Combine moved 876
barges and 512 coal boats out of the Pittsburgh harbor
for the South, a total of 24,552,000 bushels. Eight
months after starting up in business they began to work
in their own boatyards to construct 200 to 300 new coal
barges.

And thus began a phase of steamboating in America
just as peculiar in its way as rafting on the Upper Mississippi. The quantities of coal moved down the river were
prodigious. The towboats were so many you couldn't count

them and included the largest steam stern-wheel tow-boats known to man, the *Sprague*, the *Joseph B. Williams*, the *W. W. O'Neil*, and *J. B. Finley*, and others. Everything was on a colossal scale, particularly the accidents and smashups and groundings and intimate contacts with bridge piers. As a matter of record, the Combine lost, during the winter of 1903-04, not less than $189,000 as a result of the sinking of 54 loaded coal boats and 5 barges. On one trip the mighty *Sprague* alone sank a tow worth $75,000. They must have had a comfortable profit margin because they kept sending those big tows down into the bends for years and years until they lost their markets finally and for good during World War I. How they could operate and sustain their losses is a major mystery to this deck-hand.

The company suffered painfully, as told above, from accidents which involved loss of cargo. They also must surely have lost business due to the fact that the boats, to operate, depended on certain stages of the water and in low stages caused by insufficient rainfall could not operate at all. When the river remained too low to take the coal out, huge inventories were frozen in barges that accumulated by the hundreds in and around the various Combine landings at Pittsburgh. These enormous fleets of loaded coal barges sometimes lay for months at a time waiting for "coal boat water." They were made fast to enormous shore chains (some of which were dug up in 1944 in the slag bank of the P. & L. E. Railroad above the Point Bridge and exhibited as curiosities) and attended by watchmen who had to pump more or less constantly to keep these flimsy, cheaply constructed wooden craft afloat until the day of departure. For example, in February, 1904, there were 13,000,000 bushels of coal at the Pittsburgh landings waiting for higher water. In September, 1910, there were 655 barges and coal-boats loaded with 12,000,000 bushels of coal waiting for coal-boat water so they could get going to Cincinnati, Louisville, and New Orleans. In January, 1902, the Combine had 15,000,000 bushels of coal on its hands loaded and ready, and no water. (When the rise came this time the pilots struck for more pay and refused to move the coal until they got a raise.) In June, 1903, there were thirty-two Combine towboats, big stern-wheel towboats with big crews, hitched up to coal tows waiting, waiting, waiting for a rise in the river. And from June, 1903, until February, 1904, due to low water *no coal* came down the Ohio at all. When the rains came, 5,000,000 bushels of coal departed from Pittsburgh shoved by Combine towboats in twenty-four hours.

Previous to the creation of the River Combine the Pittsburgh Coal Company had been formed, joining in a like manner most of the mining properties in the district which shipped strictly by rail. This organization had attained a tremendous volume of business. On Labor Day, 1903, while the stock markets were closed, the ownership of the Monongahela River Consolidated Coal and Coke Company was transferred to the Pittsburgh Coal Company.

In these picturesque times of fifty years ago, while waiting for coal-boat water the pilots of the big steamboats used occasionally to hire a small light-draft pleasure steamer and take a trip down the river "posting up" on the channel and condition of the bars, banks, marks, and so on. With some good cigars and a plentiful supply of ham in the galley, these excursions consisting of a whole boatload of pilots were garrulous and pleasant.

The Combine continued to perform amazing feats and to entertain the whole river family with spectacular activities, but was too big and began to fall apart of its own weight. On April 30, 1916, it ceased to exist, all its assets (including the wrecked coal boats which dotted the shores of the Ohio from Sewickley to Cairo) being taken over by the Pittsburgh Coal Company. One by one the magnificent big towboats were sent to the boneyard. Here came to end their days, rotting, dirty, and falling into pathetic ruins, such glorious giants of the river as *Alice Brown, Pacific No. 2, Boaz, Tom Dodsworth, W. W. O'Neil, Raymond Horner, Wash Honshell, Voyager, Iron Age, Resolute, Coal City, Ed Roberts*, and many many others of great sentimental and historic appeal. Other boats saved themselves the humiliation of an old age in ruins and slow death by committing suicide in far-off places. The *Sam Brown* blew up, killed herself and ten men at Huntington. The *Harry Brown* sank down on the Mississippi. The *Fred Wilson* exploded her boilers, killed Captain Price and ten crew. The *Jim Wood* drowned herself down south. The *Percy Kelsey* blew her boilers. The *Defender, Joseph B. Williams*, and *J. B. Finley* all went to glory in towering flames, burning to the water. Likewise the *John A. Wood*. The *Exporter, Josh Cook, John Moren, Crusader, Relief, Tom Rees*, and *Charles Brown* all sank, total loss. A few of the boats were sold to other owners. But in

1951 the only Combine towboat left is the grand old *Sprague*, biggest and most famous of them all, spared by the grace of God and the Standard Oil Company, and owned by the city of Vicksburg, where it is to be a permanent historical exhibit. It is not in operation. Its boilers have been cold for several years.

Why did the Combine fall apart? There are as many theories about it as there are for the Decline and Fall of the Roman Empire. One of the big reasons was the constant sniping by the "Insurgents," those who refused to sell out. These included the Jutte Coal Company, Peoples Coal, United Coal, Tide Coal, Diamond Coal and Coke, Clyde Coal, Marine Coal, and others. Leaders of this faction were the Jutte Brothers, owners of some fine large towboats, and men highly skilled in the science of the river. The Insurgents stole the best pilots away from the Combine by offering them yearly contracts and high wages, and in many other ways contrived to heckle and annoy the Giant. Some say they were a big factor in the ultimate crash. The increasing use of fuel oil in the South was another thing the Combine had to fight. And the opening of coal fields nearer the southern market. And the loss of southern business during the war, when the company was ordered by the government to ship "practically all" its output to the eastern munitions plants; and the failure to recapture the southern customers again after the war. Also we might mention the high cost of operating these large towboats, and the increase of navigation hazards presented by the construction of the lock and dam system in the Ohio River. Moreover, as the industrial boom around Pittsburgh and up the Monongahela continued, there was a greatly increased demand for coal right at home.

The Combine went bust, anyway.

They quit shipping coal out of the Monongahela and the coal operators found that local industry could absorb all the coal they were able to produce. Today the big coal-towing fleets operate in the pools and to the mills on the Upper Ohio, but little coal goes downriver. The big mills with their huge by-product coke plants and other coal-gobbling enterprises are now absorbing enormous amounts from the Pittsburgh seams. After the Combine abandoned long-distance towing of coal a few of the Insurgents held on for a while, but the same changes in the scheme of things wiped them out too. The last to go was the Diamond Coal and Coke Company, which lasted until 1919. That was the end.

Chapter 15

Afternoon on the Lower Monongahela, or Captain Eternity's Soliloquy

TIME: 2:15 P.M.
PLACE: Above Lock 3, Monongahela River
SETTING: The Pilothouse of a Stern-wheel Poolboat

Captain Warren Elsey yes I ought to know Warren Elsey I worked for him long enough he was what they call the Master of Transportation for J. & L. well I think starting around 1895 or thereabouts anyway the first boat he built for them was the *Vulcan*. That was the first compound engine on the Monongahela, built in '98 or '99. I hope that boy down there in that little pushboat gets out of the way for I'm going down the river and I don't want to shove these six loads of coal up into the railroad yard to avoid running him down. Some of the dock loungers they got in these small boats around here with the title of pilot had ought to restrict their activities to pilotin' about four miles above Fairmont in a sixteen foot yawl. When I was mate on the *Boaz* we run down a skiff one night below Golconda three men was supposed to of been in it never a one of them was ever located; Captain Frank says "That shows a carefree spirit, three farmers in a homemade skiff arguing with thirty-six coal boats and the steamer *Boaz*." Move over, you dang fool, get that sand barge next to the bank. One thing we got on here is a cook who understands the fine points on a coffeepot. Here, you Joe, you ain't doing nothing but set here and keep warm, just mosey down to the galley and prevail on our good friend Mrs. Bernice to reinvigorate that pot to a certain extent. Speaking of Bernice I wonder what ever happened to that little stern-wheeler by the same name, she come down from the Upper Mississippi someplace or other she was in that rafting deal up there, a bow boat. Run up the Tennessee for quite a while seems to me she was in the big fire when the *Southland* burned up. That's more like it, junior, don't get big ideas and try to take over the whole river, we got a lot of coal here. Well I hear J. & L. is going to name the other new boat on the ways down at Dravo the *Vesta*. Rees built the first and original *Vesta* the same year the *Sprague* come out. First steel hull boat J. & L. had. Had a skeg stern on her, two skeg rudders and one balance rudder. They give that idea up when the *B. F. Jones* was built. *Vesta* was too dang narrow in the beam and turned over, flop, in a big wind after the World War at Allenport. Second *Vesta* was built down at Charleston but they renamed her the *James A. Rankin* and speak of the devil that looks like her tied up down there at the tipple.

So now they're going to move coal by pipe line I hear. After that we'll probably find somebody going into the

FIGURE 9. COAL TIPPLE AND MINE-SHAFT HOIST FRAME.

coal business by airplane or dirigible balloon. My idea is they ought to rig up some large-bore cannons and shoot the coal to its destination. They just call up the coal yard from the mine on the telephone and say "Get everybody inside, we're sending down 10,000 tons today." In a few minutes that old coal starts raining in from the sky like sixty.

Well here comes the Coast Guard, probably out checking to see if the bridges are all where they ought to be. They are good boys and they mean well but they ought to send each and every one aboard a good big coal pusher as deckhand for six months and leave them find out how much a ratchet weighs.

I *thought* that was the *Rankin*. Greetings, Mr. Joe, do me a favor and pour me out a cup of coffee. Reminds me the time I was down on the Lower Mississippi and when we turned loose and started up the river the cook found they had filled his coffee order with—*who's* that waving at us over there on the *Rankin*, Joe? Looks like Charlie—they had filled the coffee order with this here chicory coffee. Had a trip pilot aboard named Slick he just grinned from ear to ear—he *liked* it, *preferred* it you might say. Some of the strangest characters down in them parts. Like when we was up the Tennessee once, ran short of grub and Captain sent me uptown to get some supplies. Went ashore at Johnsonville, went into the General Store they had sowbelly piled up to the ceiling and an annex to hold the display of snuff. I couldn't beg borrow or buy nothing else except canned beans and Campbell's soup so I took some sowbelly back but I ate peanut butter until we got along to Sheffield

and laid in some food. So to get back to the coffee—if they
don't look out over there at that tipple why that number
416 is agoing to sink I hope the watchman is getting the
pump in her—to get back to the coffee nobody would drink
it hardly and it was wartime and we had used up our coffee
kewpons so couldn't buy no more. Got to Cincinnati and a
bunch of bankers and big shots that was directors of the
company come down to the boat for lunch to give us the
benefit of their shining faces and there was a good many
jokes passed to and fro about the coffee and an explanation
was made by the captain, the cook, the chief engineer and
the third deckhand. When lo and behold, after the dinner
one of them big Cincinnati bankers slides out to the galley.
"How much of that coffee you got?" he asks old Barrelhead
the cook. "I was raised down there," he says, "and that
chicory coffee is just like Sunday to me. I'll take the whole
lot off your hands." We had nineteen—it looks like we
might have some rain before this watch is over, look at
them ornery-looking clouds—we had nineteen pounds of
this coffee left, and he took the whole works. It takes a
lot of nutty people to make up the population of this old
globe and that's a fact. Not only that but this old boy
scouted around Cincinnati and saw to it we got nineteen
pounds of good coffee to replace it, and no kewpon discussion neither. That's what I'd like to be, a banker, Cincinnati or Pittsburgh, don't make no difference—why those
boys can do anything. WELL, can you imagine it, looks
like we're agoing to ride right into this lock on the wings
of song boys—there's the mighty steamer *Sailor* down
there leaving and it looks like we're next yes I know they

got some new name hooked onto her now since they rebuilt her, the *O'Connor* or whatever it is but she's still the *Sailor* as far as I'm concerned and in case you didn't know it she is the most powerful steam sternwheeler left here in the old Mon. And Joe, please tell that new deckhand you got out there not to scare me to death again every lock we make. Every time he throws a line he looks like he's gonna throw himself clear into space I never seen a deckhand with a fancy windup like that I keep thinkin' he's about to throw himself right off between the barge and the lock wall, mighty nerve wreckin. I guess I better give them a little solo on the whistle and let them know we are going to give them some business.

Do you see what I see, I believe they are going to let that boat coming up from below through ahead of us why he's still a mile from the lock oh but wouldn't that try the patience of the Egyptian kings. Oh these locks here on the Mon will put this old man in his grave before long, in the special six hundred dollar waterproof, fireproof and burglar proof casket with the patent handles on. Look, see them lock tenders amble down to the other end of the lock. Here, I'll give them a little more whistle music just to let them know how I feel about it. Joe, we'll slide in here and see if you can get a line out for me we'll most likely be here until a week from Thursday it looks like whoever that boat down there is he has got more tow in front of him than the *Raymond Horner*. Leave that coffee pot in the galley on the way down as a special favor will you? You know in the old days when the locks was privately owned they had a rule they wouldn't lock the coal tows through

on a Sunday here on the Mon, only packets, another case
of the high mentality of the human being, so one Sunday
down come the *William Stone* with Captain Dan McIntyre
aboard and he run right down to lock number four, blew
for the lock, and eased on in and flopped his loads right in
the way blocking the lock. Oh no they wouldn't open the
gates, said they didn't *have* to and that was the law. Said
the king of England couldn't lock no coal tow through on a
Sunday, not even if he brought the twelve apostles along
to talk for him. Said they wasn't *obliged* to, and wasn't
going to open them gates. Said he could take it to the Supreme Court but the lock gates was going to stay closed.
By and by along comes the packet *Chieftain* wanting to
lock through. No soap, McIntyre kept the lock entrance
blocked. Presently another whistle is heard from down below and the *Elisha Bennett* slows up and wants to lock
through and go places. McIntyre wouldn't budge an inch
until finally the locktender agreed to lock him through
after the packets was taken care of. So they locked a coal
tow through on a Sunday after all, and McIntyre was
no relation that I ever heard of to the English royal family
neither. The *William Stone?* Why they tell me that after
the *Arab* sank in the ice at the mouth of the Yough way
back in the Civil War days the Stone family of McKeesport
raised her and built the *William Stone* out of the wreck
for their Coal Valley Coal Company. I think in her later
days she was sold over to the Missouri River or some such
outlandish place. And speaking of ice I see the Allegheny
dumped another nice load of it into the Ohio and picked
up the *Rankin* and the *Aliquippa* and shoved them right

down on Emsworth Dam, no harm done I guess. That dang Allegheny makes and lets go of more blame ice than any crick I ever seen. I don't care for them big ice jams least of all being picked up by one and shoved up against Emsworth or any other dam. That kind of entertainment is too exciting for me I would rather go to the movies and see Wild Bill Elliot fanning his forty-five at the rustlers. Then if it gets too exciting I can go home, which is impossible when an ice jam two miles long from up around Parkers Landing is shoving the steamboat you are on right onto some dam or other. Speaking of dams reminds me of the *W. H. Warwick*. She was going downstream once upon a time and came to Ohio River lock twelve. For some reason Pilot figured the wickets were down. They were *up*. Just as *up* as possible. That didn't faze him none, he run her right over the pass, tow and all, knocked the wickets down and went on down the river. I would love to have heard them locktenders carry on.

The *J. H. McCrady* went over dam number two, right here on the romantic and historical Monongahela, back in 1913 and sank. Raised her and a couple years later she sank *again* by golly up at Braddock. They raised her again, but just because of getting into the habit of the thing she sank a third time over on the Allegheny. Up she come again, and stayed on top this time only she had a bad fire seems to me, and had to be rebuilt. Oh, she was an old-timer from back in the eighties, she was built out of an older boat, the *Traveler*, that used to be in the Allegheny oil trade in the sixties and seventies. It don't seem quite natural around these parts since they tore her down. Well

I guess we are none of us getting any younger least of all this old coal passer when I think of the way I use to make a coal scoop fly, when I think of the way I use to hustle them twenty-seven foot chains out onto the tow in a snow-storm along them four-inch gunnels—and now climbin' up them pilothouse stairs is all the work I can stand. Look at that new deckhand Joe has on the bank over there. It's his third day on a steamboat now I wonder what he'll think about it all when he's been here fifty years like me, and has made ten thousand lockings, got personally acquainted with every barge and lump of coal in the whole Mononga-hela Valley, and wasted a million hours on watch in the pilothouse talking about nothing.

Three o'clock. I imagine the cooks are laying down. JOE! Hey, Joe! Send one of the deckhands up here with the coffeepot. I wish I had one cent for every cup of steam-boat coffee I've drank on the breast of the old Mononga-hela and I'd be as rich as old Andrew or H.C. themselves. But I don't see nobody coming forward to sponsor that plan. Guess I'll set down and take the load off my feet.

Chapter 16

The Biggest of Them All

"What, you never seen the *Sprague?* Then you never seen nothin'."

You know, quite a few of the boys that write about the Lower Mississippi or in fact about steamboating in general are bound and determined to work in (*a*) those comical darkies, and (*b*) a grand conglomeration of picturesque terminology. I had read up on all this and when I got dumped on the levee a few years ago at Memphis (out of an old Illinois Central day coach from Chicago) to catch the steamer *Mackenzie* to go deckhand in the oil trade, Baton Rouge to Cincinnati, I was all ready to co-operate with the conditions down there as represented by the leading authorities.

First thing I knew up through the bridge comes the steamer *Sprague,* biggest towboat in the world, only survivor of the Combine, and according to the writers lovingly known as "Big Mama" all up and down the river. " 'Big Mama,' " they chuckle, "as she is affectionately known to the river fraternity."

There was a convenient colored man sitting on an

orange crate, so I sidled up to him and I said, "Now what big old steamboat is that, I wonder?"

According to scripture it was his cue to roll his eyes, grin from ear to ear, call for watermelon and reply, "Dat am ole Big Mama, white boy. My lans, where you ben you don' reckernize ole Big Mama asplashin' up de ribber?"

Instead, he replied:

"I told Grace I wouldn't never drink no more gin. Now I lost the rent money and here I am."

"Sure makes a pretty sight," I replied stubbornly. "Man, look at that big wheel."

"She's probly waiting for me with a meat cleaver," he said. "Too bad when a man has to sit down here and can't go to his own home and get some rest," he said, and got up and slowly walked away.

I went up and sat down on the end of a bridge timber that had got caught out on a rise. "Big Mama" was driving up through the main line. Along comes an old-timer in rubber boots.

"What's that steamboat out there?" I said, and waited for some picturesque utterance worthy of national acclaim.

"The *Sprague*," he said, and went away.

I walked up the levee and a steamboat man in store clothes was sitting on his suitcase waiting for his boat like me and rolling a cigarette. I asked him for the makings, rolled a cigarette, and looked out at "Big Mama" turning her wheel over ever so slow and walking those loads of oil up the river.

"Well, there she goes," I said, handing him back his sack of Duke's Mixture.

"Yeah," he said. "Pretty good shover."

"I come from up on the Monongahela," I said. "We don't have no big boats like that up there. What's the story on her?"

"That's the old *Sprague*," he replied. "How's everything up in the pools?"

"Not bad," I said. "Don't they have some special name they call that *Sprague?* Some nickname or other seems I heard?"

"Just the *Sprague* so far's I know. Big devil, ain't she?"

"Uh-huh," I said, discouraged, and went up to a movie as my boat was down below someplace doubletripping and wouldn't be up to Memphis for a day or more.

So that's the way it goes. You get all fired up and ready for some local color and you find out the boys haven't rehearsed their lines.

Now get this straight: the steamer *Sprague* is the biggest stern-wheel towboat ever built, and none bigger will ever be built, any more than the Egyptian government will build some bigger pyramids one of these days. Steam, on the river, is out of date. Soon it will be gone. The *Jason*, big steam stern-wheeler, was built in 1940, and it was the last stern-wheeler. During World War II the government built a bunch of very powerful twin-screw river steamers for the inland transport emergency. They were the last steam-propelled river boats built in this country and unless a miracle takes place there will be no more.

So the age of steam on the western rivers, which began

on March 17, 1811, with the launching on the Monongahela of Roosevelt's *New Orleans*, lasted about 130 years
and then began to fade away due to the damnable invention by Herr Doktor Rudolf Diesel. During this period
the art of the steamboat builder reached two sublime
heights: one was the steamer *J. M. White*, most beautiful
packet the world has ever seen (you might get an argument on that); the other was the steamer *Sprague*, biggest and most powerful stern-wheel towboat in all the
pages of history (you will not get any argument on that).

The *Sprague* was built for the Monongahela River
Consolidated Coal and Coke Company (which we know as
the Combine), was named for Captain Peter Sprague, who
was the superintendent of construction, and launched in
December, 1901. Curious to state, although the Monongahela was the cradle of western boatbuilding, and although
there were famous yards at several spots on the Ohio, the
contract for the *Sprague* was given to a shipyard out in
the corn and hog state of Iowa, on the Upper Mississippi,
over 1,500 miles away by river. The Iowa Iron Works, of
Dubuque, Iowa (now succeeded by the Dubuque Boat and
Boiler Company), got the contract and thereby squeezed
onto the pages of river history. Why the boat was built out
on the edge of the rolling prairies of the Northwest I cannot say. I don't know whether they asked for bids or what
the deal was. But, since the *Sprague* is so famous, and
loved by so many, I think it may be legal for me to set
down here some brand-new information of Big Mama that
has not before been written down except for local consumption. Reams of fact, fiction, lies, and poetry have been

written about this colossal boat but, so far as I know, nobody has ever dug up any facts on her launching.

Working for months in collaboration with a local historian in Dubuque and through bribery of high officials in the Catfish Creek Historical and Billiard Society, I have come into possession of a curious parchment called the Dubuque *Enterprise* with the strange sub-heading:

Of All That is Good Iowa Affords the Best
And Dubuque is the Key City

On page 10 of this ancient document, which is dated Sunday, December 15, 1901, appear the words: "The Humphrey GAS ARC LIGHT! The Best Light in the World. FOR LIGHTING Stores, Churches, Halls, or any large Indoor Areas. Guaranteed NOT to Consume more than 12 cubic feet of gas an hour costing, at $1.25 a thousand, $1\frac{1}{2}$ cents."

On page 11 an advertisement offers "Fancy Parlor Chairs, mahogany finished frame, rich velour covering, $4.50."

W. J. Burns Grocer offers 50 lbs. #1 flour, 99 cents. Coffee 15¢ and 20¢ lb.

Papa's Baby, the "Screaming German Musical Farce," was playing at the Opera House, following on the heels of the New York Extravaganza Company's *The City Sports*. The price schedule was:

PARQUETTE & 3 ROWS IN CIRCLE	$ .75
LAST 4 ROWS IN PARQUETTE CIRCLE	.50
BALCONY	.50 and .35
GALLERY	.25
STALLS AND BOXES	1.00

Over at the Congregational church supper you could get an oyster stew and a pickle for 5 cents. Coffee 2¢. Homemade pie 4¢.

Parker's, at 730 Main Street, offered Ladies' Drawers @ 18¢ to $1.25 and Corset Covers @ 9¢ to $1.25.

On page 3, H. A. Schunk says he will be glad to sell "whiskies, absolutely pure and wholesome" @ $1.50 and up per gallon.

The Dubuque Star Brewing Company claims that "The Star Beer Equals the Best and is Better than the Rest."

Tom Connolly sells Top Buggies from $50 and Runabouts from $55.

On page 9, Dr. Matthay insists "YOU NEED ELECTRICITY" if you are suffering from rheumatism, neuralgia, dyspepsia, kidney diseases, etc., and displays a cut of "The Wonderful Machine which creates the LIFE GIVING CURRENT."

All these items are of deep interest to the anthropologist and we record them here for further study. But we ourselves are interested in the following heading (adjoining a business notice of the Bon Ton Bakery at 1386 Clay Street):

A GREAT DAY FOR THE IOWA IRON WORKS

Hull of the Sprague, the largest towboat ever Designed, Successfully Launched—Iowa Iron Works Big Undertaking.

Here is the whole story, with two big cuts of the launching!

Here is what happened on that cold raw day of December 5, 1901, way out on the Upper Mississippi.

"In the launching of the hull of the great towboat, the P. Sprague, Thursday afternoon, it can hardly be said that she 'kissed the water,' for osculation is never accompanied by the violence with which this great hulk of 15,000 tons of steel smashed into the water. It was rather an avalanche. Its great weight, as it moved down the lubricated skids, made them smoke and there was an ominous roar as it gathered momentum. The skids, great timbers over a foot square, did not run out into the water, but projected out over the bank. The projecting ends, as the great weight shot down over them, broke as if they were pipe stems. There was the crash of the breaking timbers, followed instantly by the splash as the great hull dropped into the water. For a moment many hearing the noise of the breaking timbers, thought that something had gone amiss, but an instant later the great boat was floating majestically, and the cheer that went up gave assurance that the launching had been successful . . .

"Thousands witnessed the launching, and as many more would have been there if the axes had been stayed half an hour. In every respect the launching was a success. There was but one disappointment, and that was a most commendable and excusable one. It was that the launching was on time. It was in fact on time to the minute. It was advertised to occur at 2 o'clock, and with the striking of the hour Mr. W. W. Bonson gave the axmen the signal. Expecting that the launching would be delayed, many who intended seeing it did not hurry, and there were more people on Main street going toward the harbor at the time than there were gathered there to witness the launching. The habit of being on time, however, is characteristic of the men now at the head of the Iowa Iron Works, and they can be counted on to be there to a minute and to do just what they state they intend doing.

"Many witnessed the launching with not a little apprehension. The Sprague is the heaviest hull ever launched here, and those who saw the great swells that went rolling across the harbor from the Windom and from other boats, expected to see great havoc caused among the shipping in the harbor. A further cause for alarm among the uninitiated was that the harbor was covered with a coat of ice four inches in thickness, and it was naturally thought that this would cause further trouble.

"The sequel proved that those in charge of the launching understood the situation perfectly and had taken all precautions. The ice had been cut out where the hull was expected to strike the water, and the great swell that was sent rolling across the harbor lifted the ice like it was rubber, breaking it into chunks, but doing no damage. The great force there was seen on the south bank of the harbor, where the water falling this fall had left a lumber raft three feet on the bank. The wave was of such size that when it receded it drew the great lumber raft back with it into the water.

"Appreciating the danger there might be, particularly from the flying ice, people were cautioned not to 'go down with the boat,' and the only ones on her were Mr. Hopkins, Mr. W. W. Bonson and a half dozen employes. As the great hull crashed into the water there was a shower of ice and chunks ranging up to a foot square covering the deck.

"For the benefit of those who did not observe, a brief explanation of the method used in launching a boat may be of interest. The keel is laid on timbers built up high enough so that men can work under the boat. Over a week ago preparations were begun for the launching. First the skids were laid. These are great timbers extending down to the bank of the harbor and are firmly anchored into the sand. The cradles are built up on these skids. These cradles are heavy timbers laid one on top of the other and built up to the boat. As these cradles are built up, the timbers on which the keel was laid are taken out and in the end the hull rests on the cradles only. The upper sides of the skids are smooth, and to render the friction less are covered with grease. The cradles are built up so that the boat is held perfectly horizontal as it slides down, and it is therefore shot out over the water and drops into it. When all is ready for the launching all the supports and stays are removed so that the only fastenings are ropes bound through holes in the cradles and the upper ends of the skids. There are several strands of inch rope holding each cradle. Heavy jack-screws are set against the upper side of the boat and these start the boat so that its whole weight is on the ropes thus wound through the holes in the skids and the cradles.

"A man with a keen edged axe is stationed at the end of each skid and at the signal the axes swing in unison and sever the ropes . . .

"To look at the boat as it rests in the harbor drawing

but little over two feet of water, one cannot get an idea of its weight; in fact, it is almost impossible to realize that it weighs over 15,000 tons, or 30,000,000 pounds, yet this is its weight. This steel made over ninety car loads, more than three ordinary trains, and two full car loads of rivets have been used. The steel came here in sheets, and all the cutting and shaping, all the punching of holes for the rivets and all the rivets were driven here. To do this work the Iowa Iron Works has had between 250 and 300 men employed continuously for over four months at a weekly payroll of about $3,500, making the total amount paid for labor on the boat to date approximate $40,000.

"The work on the great boat is but fairly begun. The contract required that the Iowa Iron Works deliver the boat all ready for use and under her own steam at Cairo. This means that not only is all her upper works and all her machinery to be put on here, but also every bit of the furnishing even to the equipment of the culinary department and the furnishing of the state rooms. It is required that the boat be completed by next spring, and to accomplish this, work on her will be pushed with all the men that can be worked to advantage all winter.

"The Sprague is not only the biggest boat the Iowa Iron Works ever built but it is the biggest tow boat ever built.

"Some idea of the immense power this boat will have can be gained from an explanation of what will be required of her. She is being built for the Monongahela Consolidated Coal and Coke Company of Pittsburgh and will be used in towing coal from Louisville to New Orleans. This company now has about 15 boats engaged in this traffic, but most of them are wooden hulls and none come anywhere near the size or towing power of the Sprague.

"The Sprague is designed to tow sixty coal barges. These barges are built 170 feet long by 26 feet wide and 10 feet deep, and each will hold 26,000 bushels of coal. These coal barges are lashed together and present a solid field of coal, the surface of which is over seven acres. The barges strung out would be two miles in length, and the total amount of her tow will be 1,560,000 bushels, or 54,600 tons.

"She is expected to make the round trip from Louisville to New Orleans in thirty days, so that she will make ten to twelve trips per annum and will transport over a half million tons of coal, or over 25,000 car loads. And then some people say the railroads have killed river traffic.

"The length of the hull proper is 275 feet, and over all, including the wheel, it is 318 feet. The width is 68 feet 4 inches. The depth is 7 feet in the shallowest part, 10 feet in the bow, and 12 feet in the stern. The wheel will be 40 feet square; that is, 40 feet wide and 40 feet across, and will be the biggest wheel ever turned in the river. For months men in the Iowa Iron Works machine shops and boiler making departments have been working on the machinery and boilers that go into the boat, and have them ready now to put in place.

"There will be a battery of six of Mr. Hopkins' patented marine boilers with corrugated flues. These boilers will be each 14 feet long by 7 feet in diameter, and will have 127 flues each. The engines are monsters. The cylinders of the low pressure engines are each 63 inches in diameter. There are two high pressure and two low pressure engines. The weight of each of the low pressure engines will be in excess of 30,000 pounds.

"The propellor shaft is of nickel forged steel and is 47 feet long. It is 31 inches in diameter in the center and the hole is 21 inches.*

"There will be on the boat eight nigger engines and two doctors and much other machinery . . .

"The Sprague will have immense power. Her engines at full stroke will indicate 6,990 horse power. When it is considered that the power of the Quincy's engines is 800 horse power, some idea of the immense force the Sprague will have can be obtained. Down stream without tow she will have a speed of over twenty miles, and against the current she will make over ten miles an hour.

"The work on the boat has been done under the supervision of Capt. Peter Sprague, a veteran boat builder, who is connected with the Monongahela company, and who designed the boat. He will superintend the work that is yet to be done on her and will make the trip down the river on her. Capt. Sprague is very enthusiastic in his praise of the work on the boat and of the facilities the Iowa Iron Works has for doing this work. He also commends in the highest terms the mechanics and the work they are doing."

The *Sprague* was so long that in order to get her

* This shaft, made by the Bethlehem Steel Company, weighed 80,220 pounds.

through the Keokuk locks the boat was towed downriver minus wheel and delivered to St. Louis, where the wheel was built. She was then sent down to Cairo and entered the Combine stable (cutting down the Eisenbarth and Henderson showboat at Grand Tower on the way), where she set all-time records for tonnage and caused much conversation.

When the Combine folded, the *Sprague* was sold, in 1917, to the Aluminum Ore Company of St. Louis, and operated by them until 1925, when she was sold to the Standard Oil Company of Louisiana. While in this service, at the ripe age of 24, she took 19 loaded oil barges to Baton Rouge, containing 11,000,000 gallons; the tow was 1,123 feet long and 260 feet wide, and that is some tow. Owing to the immoral, subversive rise of the internal combustion engine, the *Sprague* was withdrawn from service in 1948. By this time she had become as famous and as much loved as the *Constitution* and a great wailing and keening went up in the Mississippi Valley that could be heard clear to the Rockies. Responding to these lamentations the directors of the Standard Oil Company (not a few of whom were themselves struggling to subdue throat lumps) presented the mighty *Sprague*, queen of all river creation, to the city of Vicksburg, to be used as a permanent historical exhibit, museum, and civic wonder. So the story ends happily.

We'll not get into hot water by attempting any full description of the career of the *Sprague* here. The shores of the Mississippi-Missouri-Ohio system are thickly populated with rivermen, both active and retired, whose hobby is writing letters to the papers explaining that the steamer *Princess* did *not* go aground on Old Man Bar but above Rocky Point and it wasn't on June 3, 1858, as reported in your columns last week, but on June 4, because the writer's great-uncle was mud clerk at the time and noted it down on a slip of paper now preserved; moreover, the *Princess* did not have the boilers out of the *Belle of Bellevue,* that was another *Princess,* which burned at Reads Landing in 1853, August 12. This kind of communication results in another letter, in a few weeks, from a retired engineer in Oregon, stating he can prove the "other *Princess*" burned at Pomeroy in 1854. So we will content ourselves with describing here what is considered the *Sprague*'s biggest feat. Skipping the date, for fear of anonymous threats, the facts are these: she took "sixty coal boats and barges, 925 feet long by 312 feet wide and covering nearly seven acres, with a cargo of 67,307 tons coal" down the Ohio and Mississippi.

That's all.

Chapter 17

Bound to Rise, or How Andy Made His Way

Andrew Carnegie, a poor boy from the squalid slums across the Allegheny known as "Slabtown," who became the richest man in the Pittsburgh area and one of the richest men in the world, was such a curious character that, although biography is not exactly our line, we cannot refrain from relating some of his story here, even if he held no pilot's license.

He came to the United States in 1848 at the age of twelve and started work as bobbin boy in the Blackstock Cotton Mill on Robinson Street in Allegheny City at a wage of $1.20 a week. At the turn of the century he possessed a fortune estimated in Wall Street at $400,000,000. Now, as anybody knows, you can't get your hooks into $400,000,000 without considerable pushing, shoving, digging of elbows, tramping on feet, wiggling and squirming, punching, clawing, use of the spikes, et cetera, but to hear him tell it in his autobiography all his maneuvers were a regular Sunday-school entertainment, and very heavy too on the poetic and cultural side. He was everlastingly writ-

ing books and going into ecstasies over the better things in
life and the advantages of honest poverty, but when you
boil it all down, making money was his game, and although it embarrassed him to admit it, at producing a dollar he was the fastest boy on the track. And while running
the risk of being called a Communist agitator, one can't
help remembering when reading his remarks on the glo-
ries of the intellectual life, and of his friendships with
Gladstone, Matthew Arnold, Herbert Spencer, and other
brilliant men, that the steelworkers at that time were living in mud, smoke, fog, soot, cinders, and filth up to their
ears. Mary Roberts Rinehart was a student nurse in one
of the Pittsburgh hospitals when a young woman and
in her autobiography she gives some violent pictures of
the daily tragedies she witnessed in the wards among the
maimed, injured, and completely disabled workers in the
steel mills and other Carnegie enterprises. This is raw
stuff. It makes tough reading. There was no compensa-
tion in those days. If you got knocked off the production
line, why, you were simply out. The old lady could try to
get work on a sewing machine for $5 a week and maybe
Nick, the eldest boy, could pick up a dollar selling papers.
It was so rugged you wonder how they made it.

As a master of double-talk the world will probably
never see Carnegie's peer. At the time of the bloody
Homestead strike, which brought the whole country down
on him in an avalanche of scorn and vituperation, he ex-
plained his position by saying that he did not come home
to Pittsburgh during the strike because his directors
wanted him to stay away, knowing that, as he cheerfully

admitted, he was such a softy that he always gave labor anything it wanted.

Of Carnegie's actions at the time of the Homestead strike, one of the most bitter conflicts between labor and capital the world has ever seen, the London *Times* had this to say: "Mr. Carnegie's position is singular. The avowed champion of trades-unions now finds himself in almost ruinous conflict with the representatives of his own views."

As for his own views, while flattering labor and cracking jokes with the workers on his infrequent visits through the mills, he was at the same time laying out a comprehensive and violent campaign for completely smashing the unions. And, curiously enough, while the workers were trying to contact him direct, to persuade him to cancel the plan of H. C. Frick, his plant manager and fall guy, to reopen the mills with nonunion labor, he had retreated to a lonesome lodge in his beloved Scotland, thirty-five miles from railroad and telegraph, as inaccessible as if he had been in a balloon.

Tough? Hard boiled? For a lover of the birds and bees and high-toned literature he was certainly handy with the brass knuckles.

Yet all the time he was telling himself that his ideals were as high as the Matterhorn. At the age of thirty-three, already with an income of $50,000 a year, he sat down one night in the Hotel Nicholas in New York and penned himself a memorandum to the effect that $50,000 a year was enough for any man and that from now on he should "make no effort to increase fortune but spend the surplus each year for benevolent purposes. *Cast aside business forever* [my italics] . . . the amassing of wealth is one of the worst species of idolatry—no idol more debasing than the worship of money," etc. etc.

These are noble sentiments and having written them down he entered in the next twenty years upon a career of rate cutting, violation of pool agreements, secret rebates, knifing of competitors, whiplashing of associates and underlings, and general money grabbing that was truly incredible. And all the time telling funny stories at the dinner table, reeling off yards and yards of Shakespeare and Robert Burns, beaming and chuckling, reading omnivorously, and having Great Thoughts such as "labor is the universal law of being" and "I would prefer to have my niece marry an honest working man than a worthless duke," doing card tricks, and in truth entertaining both himself and his friends in a vivacious manner. No question about his charm; he could hypnotize devil and saint alike. No question either that in him a wild lust for dividend checks was waging a battle (and ever winning) with his desire to "settle in Oxford and get a thorough education, making the acquaintance of literary men."

He never ceased to issue proclamations of "virtuous austerity" while at the same time he was undoubtedly the most ravenous and ruthless schemer American industry has ever known. This split in his personality reveals the innocence of the man.

He stood five feet four inches from the ground and was made of kiln-dried hickory, or maybe lignum vitae. And as one of his biographers says, "His head was round and big and hard and Scotch and full of brains." His first patron, Colonel Thomas A. Scott of the Pennsylvania Railroad, called him "that little white-haired Scotch devil of mine." Down among the blast furnaces he was called other names. His superintendent, Captain William R. Jones, is responsible for the oft-quoted remark that "Andy was born with two sets of teeth and holes bored for more."

The only man in Pittsburgh, maybe anyplace, who ever got the best of the terrifying little Scot was H. C. Frick, the King of Coke, whose fabulous mansion still stands on Fifth Avenue in New York, and who was just as acquisitive and just as tough as Andrew Carnegie himself. Frick controlled the Connellsville coke industry, which fed the mills at Pittsburgh, and on this he thrived mightily. Soon a deal was made and Carnegie and Frick joined forces. Frick's talent for organization and his terrific drive did not escape Carnegie's eye, and seven years later Frick was in supreme command of all the properties along the Monongahela, while the boss was more and more free to live a life of "culture" abroad. Frick's management of the company was phenomenally successful, so successful in fact that Carnegie's nose got out of joint and he began to pick a fight with him. With a Machiavellian skill second to none he began to drop remarks about Frick to various associates, obviously with the intention that they would get back to his pal.

They did. But Frick didn't run and hide under the porch. Hell, no. He was a 30-minute hard-boiled egg himself and in addition was an out-and-out cynic, not wasting any time in spouting the mushy morality in which Carnegie wallowed incessantly.

To the astonishment and horror of the other directors, at the next meeting of the board Mr. Henry Clay Frick addressed a formal communication reading in part as follows:

"Mr. Carnegie stated, I am told, while here that he had purchased that land from me above Peter's Creek; that he had agreed to pay market price, although he had his doubts as to whether I had any right, while chairman of the Board of Managers of the Carnegie Steel Company, to make such a purchase. He knows how I became interested in that land, because I told him so in your presence, the other day. Why was he not manly enough to say to my face what he had said behind my back? He knew he had no right to say what he did. Now, before the Steel Company becomes the owner of that land, he must apologize for that statement . . .

"Harmony is so essential for the success of any organization that I have stood a great many insults from Mr. Carnegie in the past, but I will submit to no further insults in the future."

Now, *nobody* ever talked like that to Andrew Carnegie.

When Andrew received the minutes of the meeting in New York and read them he blew his stack a mile high and the fight was on. He immediately had Frick bounced and then tried to force Frick to sell out his stock to the company "at book value," which Carnegie figured at $4,900,000. In view of the fact that Frick's shares were earning more than this amount annually, we are not surprised to find that he refused.

John K. Winkler describes the ensuing battle in *Incredible Carnegie:* "In March, Frick filed an equity suit. The complaint and Carnegie's answers were bitter and abusive. Frick called Carnegie a fraud and a cheat, animated by personal hatred. Carnegie retorted in kind. Frick, he swore, was 'a man of ungovernable temper.' Belaboring each other like enraged washerwomen, the great leaders of industry furnished an edifying spectacle. The quarrel and its consequent revelation of the stupendous profits of the Carnegie Company, hitherto suspected but never proven, attracted world attention. Here was the responsible manager of the firm swearing that the value of its assets, as of December 31, 1899, was no less than a quarter of a billion dollars—ten times its capitalization.

"Everywhere pages were printed of the 'secrets of the Steel Trust.' Editors and legislators expressed the hope the case would go to trial. One journal declared: 'What legislative bodies and committees of inquiry have failed to accomplish may be reached if the secrets of the great corporation are passed in review through the courts.' At every cross-roads people discussed the evils of bloated tariff-protected monopolies. Angry murmurs came from the great army of Carnegie workmen, laboring twelve hours a day, some of them seven days a week, to pile up these unshared profits. The common man had a new Octopus to curse. Temporarily, John D. and his wicked Standard Oil Company were forgotten."

Frick, now twice as angry as his former boss, threatened to produce a carload of TNT at the trial in the form of an imprudent letter by Charlie Schwab exposing the Carnegie profits and showing that tariff protection was no longer necessary for the American steel industry. The Old Man gave in and called off the fight. In the end, instead of the $4,900,000 which was Carnegie's settlement offer, Frick received, two years later, securities of the newly organized United States Steel Corporation with a market value of $25,000,000.

In his sixty-sixth year Carnegie finally did quit business, thirty-three years late on the Employees' Timetable he had written up for himself in the Hotel Nicholas that night in 1868. He had run his $50,000 into $400,000,000. At this point he retired, and spent the rest of his life giving his money away. And now, having lambasted him for several pages, we must admit that this leopard did change his spots and became in thought and deed a true benefactor of mankind. All the noble sentiments that he had been issuing for years on the public obligations of the wealthy he now put into immediate practice. He blossomed and overflowed with genuine goodness. Maybe he had meant what he said about the "disgrace" of extreme wealth and the virtues of "honest poverty." After hacking his way with a machete through the jungle of railroads, steel, coke, ore, and Wall Street in a frenzy of money grabbing, he donned the robes of charity and gave away exactly $350,695,653.40 before going to join his ancestors.

Chapter 18

The Terrifying Western River Steam Boiler

Everybody has heard about the fancy dinner menus on the old-time steamboats and nearly everybody knows about the gingerbread on the pilothouse and the aristocratic ways of the pilot. All the lore of packet days has been fully exploited and almost anybody can tell you about gamblers and fancy ladies, and the lights that sparkled in the long saloons, and the oil paintings on the stateroom doors. Everybody knows all about these things, but few know what made the boats go.

The steam boiler was doing all the work and the pilot in his kid gloves was taking all the credit. While the pilot smoked a good Wheeling stogie and entertained the ladies with lies and samples of his profile, the old boilers down there on the main deck were working fit to bust (and sometimes did bust) with nobody for company but a couple of engineers and some firemen in dirty jeans. Nobody introduced them to any of the ladies and nobody came to wonder and praise them for their energy and devotion to the cause.

Early steam boilers were rectangular and put together with bolts, with gaskets to give them tightness. They were good for pressures up to 25 pounds, but there has been a steady increase in boiler pressures and they will probably someday get above 2,000 pounds, if they haven't already. When they get up much above that, the boilers will be all tubes and probably without drums at all, or maybe we'll be all finished with steam. Actually we are pretty nearly finished with steam right now. There were about sixty or seventy new boats built in 1950 for the river interests, all of them diesel; not one new steam-propelled river boat slid down the ways in any American shipyard. This is a sad thing to have happen in our time, but the owners of modern towing fleets are not interested in perpetuating picturesque customs so much as they are in lowering operating costs, and the engineers tell us the answer is diesel engines. To those of us who have always been fascinated by the crude, elemental grandeur of steam the passing of the steamboats is causing many heartaches.

Despite constant improvements in boiler construction, the western rivers were enlivened throughout the nineteenth century by the sound of boiler explosions. According to *De Bow's Review*, dated 1848, up to that time there had already been over 230 steamboat explosions. Most of these are described with great relish and in gory detail in *Lloyd's Steamboat Directory*, printed in Cincinnati in 1855.

What was the cause of boiler explosions on the river steamboats? Some say pure carelessness, but this cannot explain the occasions on which some of the most careful and

FIGURE 10. THE *Sprague* ("BIG MAMA"), LARGEST STERN-WHEEL
TOWBOAT ON WESTERN RIVERS. BUILT FOR MONONGAHELA CONSOLI-
DATED COAL & COKE CO., 1901.

conscientious engineers in the business suddenly found themselves flying through the air to land across the river in the top of a cottonwood tree. Charles Edward Russell, an Upper Mississippi riverman, has this to say of boiler explosions:

"But the blame hardly lodged against the engineers of that period. For a long time after the introduction of steam machinery all of it was crude, unscientific, and largely experimental. The boilers were of iron, the water gauge protection was faulty; of the vast, accurate, and truly admirable volume of knowledge of steam and its ways that we now have, almost nothing was collected. Sometimes it was possible after the event to learn why the boilers had exploded; sometimes no human ingenuity could cope with that problem. Sometimes the boilers blew up while the boat was soberly and dutifully making her way along, sometimes they exploded while the boat was lying peacefully at the levee, and both varieties seemed for a long time equally mysterious."

Undoubtedly one of the chief causes was letting the water get too low in the boilers, which exposed the plates until red hot, then throwing in water and instantaneously jumping the steam pressure faster than the engines or safety valves could release it. Then followed the inevitable giving way of the entire fabric of the boiler, accompanied by a noise like the thunder of doom, and to the accompaniment of a rush of death-dealing live steam the wooden superstructure of the boat was torn to bits while fragments were thrown half a mile into the air.

These oft-repeated sound effects of the western valleys

reached a grand climax in the explosion of the steamer *Sultana* in April, 1865, a big noise that killed 1,228 persons, the worst disaster of all time on the western waters. This blowup was caused by leaky boilers.

One of George Byron Merrick's priceless remarks about piloting is about boilers. He says: "The pilot's answer to the question whether the boiler water is below the safety point comes as he feels the deck lifting beneath his feet and he sails away to leeward amid the debris of a wrecked steamboat."

Comparatively few people who "sailed away to leeward" in this manner lived to tell about it. A Mr. H. A. Kidd, however, has recorded this experience in a piece curiously entitled "The Experience of a Blown-Up Man."

Mr. Kidd was the editor of the New Orleans *Crescent* and was invited on the new and beautiful steamer *Anglo-Norman* on December 14, 1850, on an "experimental trip." A large pleasure party was aboard—over two hundred people. The boat handled beautifully, the guests enjoyed themselves thoroughly, and the owners were blushing with pride and the prospects of a long and profitable career, when all the boilers exploded at the same instant, shattering most of the boat and killing and wounding nearly half the people aboard. Mr. Kidd says:

"Mr. Bigny, one of the editors of the 'Delta' and myself, took the only two chairs remaining unoccupied on the deck; his chair having the back towards the pilot house, and mine with its back to the chimney. It will be seen at once that we had seated ourselves immediately over the monster boilers of the boat.

"We had been engaged in conversation but a very few minutes, when a jet of hot water, accompanied with steam, was forced out of the main pipe just aft the chimney, and fell near us in a considerable shower. I had never noticed anything of the kind before, and thought the occurrence very extraordinary. Just as I was about remarking this to Mr. Bigny, I was suddenly lifted high in the air, how high it is impossible for me to say. I have a distinct recollection of passing rather irregularly through the air, enveloped, as it seemed to me, in a dense cloud, through which no object was discernible. There was a sufficient lapse of time for me to have a distinct impression on my mind that I must inevitably be lost. In what position I went into the water, and to what depth I went, I have not the slightest idea. When I arose to the surface I wiped the water from my face, and attempted to obtain a view of things around me, but this I was prevented from doing by the vapor of steam, which enveloped every thing as a cloud. This obscuration, however, lasted but a short time, and when it had passed away, I had a clear conception of my situation. I found myself in possession of my senses, and my limbs in good working order. I looked around in every direction, and discovered that I was not far from the center of the river, and in the neighborhood of some twenty or thirty people, who seemed to have been thrown into the water somewhat in a heap. They were sustaining themselves on the surface as best they could, many of them endeavoring to get possession of floating pieces of the wreck. I could see nothing of the exploded boat, and was fully satisfied in my mind that she was blown all to pieces, and that all

my fellow passengers were lost, except those who, like myself, were struggling in the water. I will do myself the
simple justice to say that, from the time at which I had
arisen to the surface, I had no apprehension of drowning,
though to a more disinterested spectator the chances might
have appeared to have been against me. I never felt more
buoyant, or swam with greater ease. Still I thought it well
enough to appropriate whatever aid was within my reach;
so like others, I began a race, which proved to be a tedious one, after a shattered piece of plank. I finally reached
it, and putting my hands rather rudely upon it, I got a
sousing for my pains. The piece was too small to render
me any material service. I abandoned it, and turned in
the direction of a steamboat, which I perceived advanc-
ing toward us. To keep my face towards the approaching
steamer, I found that I had to oppose the strong current
of the river. This, together with the coldness of the water,
so exhausted my physical energies, that, for a brief space,
I felt that I should not be able to keep afloat until the boat
should reach me. As the steamer came near, there was a
cry from my unfortunate neighbors in the water. 'Stop the
boat! stop the boat!'

"There was, indeed great danger of our being run
over by it. I had, however, no fears on this point, and made
no effort to get out of its way. Fortunately for myself, I
was one of the first which the boat approached. A sailor
threw out to me a large rope, which I succeeded in grasp-
ing at the first effort. I was drawn to the boat's guards,
which was several feet above the water. While drawing
me up, the kind-hearted sailor cried, 'Hold on, partner!

hold on!' But I could not, my strength being exhausted, the rope was slipping through my hands, and I should certainly have fallen back into the water, and been irrecoverably lost under the boat's guards, had not another sailor quickly reached down and seized hold of my arms. I was drawn on board as nearly lifeless as any one could be without being actually dead. Two stout men assisted me to reach the cabin. My chest as I discovered from its soreness and my spitting of blood, had been somewhat bruised, but a little bathing with whisky soon gave me relief. My friend Bigny was one of the first I met on board."

Back in 1817, Oliver Evans, the man who introduced the cylindrical boiler in the United States and whose son George had an engine-building establishment at Pittsburgh, had said in *Niles' Register:* "Citizens attend! Surely the sum of death and misery occasioned by the explosion of the boilers of steam engines on the boats is now enough to arrest your attention, if you ever intend to travel on steamboats." He then goes on to prove that these boilers, which he claims to have invented, could "not be exploded." But, as Gould says in his *History of River Navigation*, "Later experiences show that Evans was sadly mistaken."

For example, there was the *Moselle*. She blew to eternity in 1830 taking 150 souls with her. The captain was a smart aleck who liked to load down his safety valve under the impression that he had special boiler dispensation from the Almighty.

Or the *Clipper*. In 1843 she "blew up with a report that shook earth, air and heaven, as though the walls of the world were tumbling to pieces around our ears. All the boilers burst simultaneously; vast fragments of machinery, huge beams of timber, articles of furniture, and human bodies, were shot up perpendicularly, as it seemed, hundreds of fathoms in the air, and fell like the jets of a fountain in various directions, some dropping on the neighboring shore, some on the roofs of the houses, some into the river, and some on the deck of the boat. Some large fragments of the boilers, etc., were blown at least two hundred and fifty yards from the scene of the destruction."

Actually a number of reasons in addition to the crudeness of the machinery itself may be given for the constant cannonading of bursting boilers in the nineteenth century. The public's desire for speed, the competitive spirit and pride of the commanding officers, combined with a high incidence of ignorance and negligence on the part of engineers and engine-room personnel undoubtedly were the direct causes of many tragedies.

In addition to being less than perfect in the matter of safety, the western river steamboat was also inefficient in the matter of its boilers and engines. Before the invention of the "doctor," or independent boiler feed pump, the boiler water was supplied by a pump attached to the crosshead; it was sometimes necessary, when the boiler water ran low, to make a landing, disconnect the paddle wheels, and run the engine at high speed until the boilers were filled. And the chief objection by steamboat interests to the introduction of the "doctor" pump was its cost: $600.

Also, until as late as 1850, few western river boilers

were provided with steam pressure gauges. In other words, the engineer had no idea other than from the sound of the exhaust, the pulse of the engines working, and the look and sound of the steam escaping from the try cocks, as to how much steam he was carrying.

In this connection John Wallace, who published *The Practical Engineer* in 1853, reports the following hair-raising facts: "I recollect a first-rate engineer telling me that when he was on the river he applied a straight-edge to the back boiler heads, and every time the engine would take steam, the boiler heads would spring in, and then out, from ⅛ to ¼ inch. John Warden, early Pittsburgh engine builder, said he had seen large low pressure boilers, on the Great Lakes, panting on the sides. Every time the steam was let into the cylinder, the sides of the boiler would shrink in, and when the valve was shut they would swell out constantly whilst the engine was running —just the same as a man's chest heaving in and out every time he breathes, inhaling and exhaling the atmosphere." Imagine a situation like that, and not knowing how much steam was being carried.

A nineteenth-century engineer from the East named Kent, with the classical engineering training of his time, says: "If you consider the purpose of engineering, as the marine engineers do . . . then the Western river boats are as far away from it as they can possibly get; they are terribly expensive in fuel; they are very cheap; they are clumsily constructed; they have a stroke six times the diameter of the cylinder; they have a very slow stroke and great condensation of steam, and everything else that is bad."

A popular horror story on the river is the one about the fireman who was sealed up in the boilers by mistake after the periodic cleanout. This unfortunate person is supposed to have been trapped inside while the engineer pumped up the boilers, the fires were lit, steam was made, and the fireman was only missed after the boat had made a hasty departure and was bowling up the river. The above-quoted Wallace says: "As to the particulars, I never have heard much, as it was a rather delicate matter to say much about." However of one man who did get shut up in a boiler, Wallace gives us these details: "He was at the front end, and one of the gauge cocks happening to be out, he whistled through the gauge cock hole, and was heard by someone on the boat, who immediately gave the alarm and the man-plate was taken off and he came out. His name was John Scott, engine builder, Pittsburgh."

Chapter 19

Night Watch on the Upper Monongahela

"Don't say another word, boy. I been there and I know just what you mean."

So you are dreaming a dream and you are down at the old pool hall at home having a game with some of the boys and drinking beer—man, it's cozy in there with the pool balls clicking in that sweet musical way and the boys kidding each other. Outside on Sixth Street it's raining and you can kinda sense the swishing of wet rubber as the cars slide past.

"Where you goin' tonight, Eddie?"

"Got a date with Lucille. We'll probably end up at the Royal, I suppose, man, that girl goes through a pair shoes a week. I never went with no girl so cracked on the subject of dancing as her."

So then the dream shifts scenery and you are in that old '35 Ford you used to have with the bum flywheel ring gear and Fritzie Wentgill is in your arms; you haven't

204

thought of Fritzie, the high school bad girl, for eleven years but this is Fritzie all right and she flutters her long lashes like Sue Carol and you say:

"Fritzie, I always knew we were destined for this. Darling, remember the night of the Hi-Y dance in sophomore year?" You are about to drop into a regular movie kiss, you can smell the perfume of her curly bobbed hair, she's melting in your manly embrace.

And she says:

"11:45 CAP TIME TO GET UP CAP IT'S 11:45 WE'RE RIGHT ABOUT LOCK 11 COMING DOWN ARE YOU AWAKE CAP?"

Good-bye, Fritzie. Good night, sweetheart. Till we never meet again. Good-bye, dream—farewell, youth.

"YEAH, I'M O.K."

Arise, worker of the world. Get up, you crazy bum.

While sitting on the bunk pulling on your romeos you wonder what side of the family this madness comes from that makes you live like this.

"It's romantic. That's what I like about steamboatin', the romance of the blame thing," says the engineer, pulling on his pants.

"Me too," you say. "Most romantic evenin' so far I ever put in."

"Lovely romantic odor of American Beauty roses in this here bunkroom, too."

"Uh."

You step out of the bunkroom. By God, that air wakes you up in a hurry. Cold, man, what a cold frosty night and the moon never in sight. So you go down to the galley and get a cup of coffee. The deckhand is sitting there eating a piece of bread. The engineer cuts a slice of salami.

"More romance," he says. "Salami."

You go out and up the deck and climb the steel steps to the pilothouse, slide open the door and go in. Duke is there, he's been sitting there in that little room for six hours and he's ready for a change.

"Go and lay down for six hours, Duke, and have some happy dreams of a land where there ain't any coal barges."

He's just going off watch and he feels swell. You're just going on watch and you feel mean and miserable and half dead and he knows just how you feel.

"Hello, Beedle. How'd you like to be back in old Chicago, kid, settin' in the 606 or the L. & L. with some doll? How'd you like to hear them trains over your head on Wabash Avenue tonight, boy? And room 1624 at the Stevens with a view of the boulevard and a big tile bathroom. You know, Beedle, in them Chicago hotels the bath towels is two inches thick. 'Hello, Room Service? Me and the little lady is in need of refreshment. Send up two turkey sangwidges on white, a bottle of Old Hickory, some soda and a bucket of ice. Yeah. And a couple of good cigars. And the newspapers. And a couple movie magazines for the doll. Yeah. Yeah, that's all.' Yeah, man, Beedle, that's that old Chicago for you, kid."

"I'd settle for Pittsburgh tonight. They got trains, and dolls, and hotels down there too. But beat it before you get a leg broke."

"You got her, kid. Call for orders when you get in. I imagine the man'll send you down to Rosedale."

Duke goes out and then he sticks his head back in again.

"If you see any pretty scenery along the way be sure to wake me up. I don't wanna miss nothin' educational on this excursion."

"I'll do that."

It's five minutes past midnight. You're above Lock 11 coming down with one load. You'd know it anyway, even if the deckhand hadn't said so. You know from the shape of the hills that you're right abreast of the Upper Black buoy at Grassy Island. Pretty soon the lights of the lock will come into sight down by the point. Duke and you never go through that formality of saying where you are when relieving each other. Unless running in a fog.

After Duke leaves it's lonesome. You want somebody to help you cuss the company and steamboating in general. You hold her down the shore and drink your coffee and light a cigarette. That's better.

You lock down through.

"Fine time to get a man out in the night air," shouts the lockman.

"I feel terrible sorry about you, Harry," you reply, leaning out of the pilothouse.

Then you leave and run down around the bend and blow for the landing and you pull on the light, write in the log: "1:10 Arrive Dupont drop one load. Call for orders," and kick the indicator to Slow. After you get tied up you climb down out of the pilothouse and walk across the fleet of coal barges and climb up the ladder to the landing.

It's a mountain of coal. Thousands of tons. They make some by-product out of it, nobody knows exactly what.

The landing watchman comes out with a complicated speech, the same one he makes every time. It's friendly and touched with humor but he's talking Welsh, a language you don't understand.

"You're right, pal," you say. "Lots of coal and life is wonderful. Seen anything of Dylan Thomas lately?"

He replies with great good spirits in Welsh. He is a huge man, probably from the collieries at Pontypridd, Llwehwr, or Caerphilly.

He chuckles and gestures toward the barges, row on row below in the silent river.

You tread carefully in the coal which is the earth under your feet toward the telephone, hidden beneath a pile of steel.

It's delightful to call the shore agent and wake him up at 1:30 A.M. Well, we're awake and giving our all for the company. It is delicious to pluck him from his warm bed and make him suffer a little.

"Take two empties," he says, half awake. "Drop one at Arkwright. Drop the other at Rosedale. Pick up a load at Rosedale. Deliver to Dupont. Pick up one empty and make a trip to Kingmont and bring down two. Drop one at Jordan and bring the other one in."

"I got that O.K. But see here, I got a grocery order to give you."

"Tomorrow. Call it in tomorrow," he groans.

Back in the pilothouse you write in the log: "1:35 A.M. Depart down 2 MT's." You face up and turn loose and the diesel hits it and in a minute the lights fade behind you.

You double-lock through number 10. Depart down 2:20.

Passing town you look at the lights. You can see the street lights and as you pass the side streets running down to the river you can look up them toward Main Street. One or two neon lights show where the all-night lunch and a tavern are still open. You look at the dark houses and think of the guys and dolls and kids asleep in them. Where there's a light on, you wonder is it a poker game in the kitchen, mama waiting up for papa to come home from the lodge, or maybe somebody warming up the baby's bottle. You think of home and you feel like hell and you slide under the bridge—another night watch. You wonder if your brother bought that new gun and what they're doing in the old home town tonight.

The twinkling lights of the town are beautiful and you're a hero. A pilot! What you dreamed of as a kid. The river is dark and mysterious, but it's your baby, you know it like a poem. You're the big cheese, it's all up to you. No make-believe. It's a real pilothouse and you're The Man.

But you don't feel any of these things. You're sour on life. It's a mess. The stockholders are laying around drinking champagne but you're a slave, dirty and alone in the dirty night.

"I'm through," you say out loud. "My last watch! To-

morrow I go up the bank for good. A job for crazy people!
No, thanks. Four more hours and I'm done." You feel
better.

It's something you go through between midnight and
3:00 A.M. every morning. Every morning you quit the river
for good. But the next night you're still here and you
quit all over again.

The engineer comes in the door.

"Here," he says. "I brung you some coffee."

"I was just thinking of it," you say. "Thanks."

"You know what I'm gonna do when I quit?" he says.
"I'm gonna get me a big framed picture of this here boat
with a light over it that lights it up real good. Then I'm
gonna set my alarm clock for 1:00 A.M. every night and
I'm gonna have it hooked up so when that alarm goes off it
lights up the picture. I'm gonna wake up every night
when she goes off and look at that picture of this miserable kerosene burner and I'm gonna laugh and laugh and
laugh. I'm gonna wake up Marie and say 'Look, honey, it's
me, I'm home. I ain't on that dang old boat, I'm right
here. Tonight and every night.' Then I'm gonna laugh
some more and turn off the light and go to sleep."

"Marie's gonna get tired of that routine," you say.

"No, she ain't. She'll put up with anything just to
have me home with her and the kids."

"I think I'll rig me up something like that too," you
say. "When I quit."

"Yeah, when we quit," he says, and goes back to look
at the engine.

2:30 A.M. The deckhand limps out on the barges and

you flank in to the tipple and drop an empty, trying to keep the stern out of the mud.

You snap on the light and log it: "2:30 A.M. Arrive Arkwright. Drop #18. 2:40 A.M. Depart down one MT, for Rosedale."

You go on down the river. You whistle for a while. You whistle all those tunes they used to play out at the Royal Dance Palais when you were in high school and wore a blue serge suit. You wonder what happened to Marge. And Spud Hanson, the football hero, now he's driving a cab. You light a cigarette but it tastes rotten and you slide back the window and flick it out; it sails in a long arc and disappears in the Monongahela.

You hate to do it but you reach up and blow two short blasts on the whistle.

Pretty soon the deckhand shows up, eating an egg sandwich.

"What you want, cap?" he says.

"Come on in and shut the door," you say. "I want some company."

He slumps against the door and eats. He says nothing.

"So you don't think much of this deckhand racket, hey?" you say. "Well, boy, it's all in how you feel about it."

"I don't feel nothin' about it except tard and sleepy most of the time."

"You ain't hungry, anyway. I bet you never ate like this before, now, did you?"

"No I can't say I did. My ma died when I was a squirt

and my sister is suppose to be the cook when she ain't down at the tavern."

"Now about deckin' on a steamboat. Here I'm a pilot now, something I never dreamed I could ever get to be. You know some guys want to be on the state legislature and some want to be famous surgeons, but what I always thought was the grandest thing in the world from the time I was just a kid over there on the Mississippi was a steamboat pilot. God knows why. It's just one of those crazy ideas a guy gets. And now here I am. And you know something? Aside from the wages I'd change with you in a minute. Look at you, all you got to do from now until 6:00 A.M. is stand here and listen to me or go down and set in the galley or once in a while make a lock or a landing. And don't you like the feel of that lock line in your hand? Don't you like that coal crunching under your feet? Don't you feel proud when you stand out there on the head of a barge coming into a lock or landing breathing in all that fresh air? Why, man, you're just like Tom Mix riding into some cow town on Tony the Wonder Horse."

"I never noticed none of them feelings yet."

"Stick to the river awhile and you will. You're probably homesick."

"That ain't no lie. I'd like to be home right now."

"Stick around, kid. You go home first thing you know you'll end up in a coal mine and then where'll you be?"

"Underground."

"Oh, I admit this ain't much of a boat and it's kind of a tiresome run, but you can learn some deckin' here just the same. And then you can go down to Pittsburgh and get on one of them big boats and go down the river. Man, the sights you'll see. Why, Cincinnati at night looks like sixteen carnivals all rolled into one. And then you'll come into that big old mean Mississippi and slide on down past Memphis, and Helena, and Vicksburg, right to New Orleans. Wait till you see New Orleans, boy, you'll forget about that old coal camp up in West Virginia. When you come home you'll go into the tavern and say 'Oh, yas, we just brought eight loads of high-test gas in from Baton Rouge. Pretty high water down around Memphis.' You'll be a killer around there, kid. And say, the first time you go into the engine room on one of them big stern-wheelers and see all that brass and paint and big white steam lines, and them pitmans as big as a pine tree, why, your eyes will stick out like you was in Paris, France. Why, hell, boy, this steamboatin' is the most beautiful thing that was ever invented."

"You tell it good, but we ain't goin' to Cincinnati on this here outfit."

"Listen, don't talk like a squarehead. I keep tellin' you, you got a wonderful chance here to learn the game before you move on down to them big rivers."

"Just how in the hell can you see where we're goin' without no light on, will you tell me that?"

"Because I know right where I am. I been over this dang stretch so much I could run it half dead in an oxygen tent. Now go down and bring me up some more coffee."

Bye and bye you blow for the Star City ferry. It

doesn't run at night but maybe the whistle will wake somebody up, make somebody happy or sad to hear it winding up the runs, bouncing off the hills. Maybe some West Virginia genius will write a poem, jump out the window, or decide to make new friends when he hears that plaintive note on the night air.

The engineer comes back.

"Here, hold her for me while I go get some smokes," you say. "Just hold her easy off the shore. Use the light if you want."

In the darkness of the bunkroom Duke's cigarette is glowing.

"Can't you sleep on her?" you say.

"Not tonight. Can't sleep on her somehow." His voice comes to you out of the sweaty dark—clear and calm and sleepy.

Back in the pilothouse the engineer says, "Somebody comin' up. I seen a light down in the bend."

"I don't see no light now."

"He's a-comin' just the same."

"Maybe the ghost of the *Adam Jacobs*."

"What's that?"

"Packet that run up in here about a hundred years ago."

"More like the *Reliance* on the way to Fairmont with oil, I'd say."

"Well, I s'pose you better get down in the engine room, anyways."

"Yeah, I s'pose."

He stands in the door.

"Duke can't sleep on her," you say, informative, conversational.

"That's steamboatin'. Them on watch wants to sleep. Them off watch lays in the bunk worryin' about life and can't sleep. I wonder what life on the railroad is like."

He goes away.

You turn on your searchlight and angle it up in a long beam into the sky pointing downstream. You arc it back and forth slowly and switch it off. If there's another boat down there around the bend and out of sight he'll answer. You wait awhile. And no answer.

Then suddenly there's his beam. Out of the darkness and the mystery downriver the other pilot, another member of the tribe of us desperate characters who run the river at night, shoots up a beam that is both a warning signal and a greeting.

"Whoever you are, here we come," it says. "Greetings, fellow stargazer. And how is everything going up in your pilothouse tonight?"

Pretty soon you see him coming around the bend. When he's a mile away you flash him a signal; you flip your light on, then off. "Pass on the right."

But he doesn't like this. He sends back a signal: On, off, on, off. "Pass on the left." Oh, well, it makes no difference to you, with one lone empty and this little towboat, where you run. It's somebody coming up with loads, most likely the *Reliance*, like the engineer said, and he's got some reason for where he wants to go.

You give him back two. Then you give him two on the whistle. You start to shape over for a left pass. You open the window to see if you can tell who it is by the whistle. Faintly drifting upstream you hear a dying note of a steam whistle. Then again. You decide definitely it's the *Reliance*. That's the only nondiesel boat that ever ventures up here into the wilderness.

Then pretty soon you can see the red and green running lights on his tow and he's coming up the east shore. You're in good shape, and still plenty of water. You're forty feet off the red buoy.

You pass down alongside his barges very fast, and then there's the big white steamboat, a couple of deckhands on the guard, an engineer leaning out the door of the engine room, and you give them a nasal blat with your air horn and turn on the pilothouse light and wave over. Up in the big pilot house the other pilot turns on his light and waves across. And the steam whistle, ah, you can't imitate that in print. He gives you a short one that sends shivers up your spine, you on this oil-burning old tugboat. You're about to swoon, you grab for the smelling salts. Again! He gives you another note that trails off into a whoosh of steam and poetry.

But now he's gone. You see the stern and the pitman and the wheel and the waterfall and the spray in the stern lights and then you're all alone in the black again, and you dream an old, old dream of real steamboats. For there's never in the world anything like the sound of steam boilers, never anything like the smell in the engine room of a real steamboat, nor anything like the majesty of those two big horizontal engines with the crossheads moving to and fro as smooth as silk and the pitman rising and falling with the authority of power. It's all so beautiful you choke up like in the movies and you think: I'm part of it. Low miserable skunk that I am, pilot on this decrepit excuse of an old clunker with its lousy internal combustion. I'm hanging on the coattails of the beautiful art of steamboating but I'm here, I'm here on this river, not selling hardware or demonstrating washing machines.

You're over the 3:00 A.M. hump. Everything looks grand. You sit and take her on down and you think of a million wonderful things. You feel like jumping in the river and swimming right on down to the bottom and digging your hands in that sand and mud.

But here you are at Rosedale. No lights. They don't ever put out lights on the coal landings up here in the sticks. You ring for a slow bell; you pretend you're dropping in here with a fleet of eighteen mixed loads and empties instead of this one old beat-up standard. It's the *John W. Hubbard* instead of the old *Coal Queen* and you've got a mate and four deckhands out there on the fleet instead of one stray from a mine village. You drop her against the pilings with only two bells and while the deckhand is tying off you jump down out of the brain box and knock the face wires loose.

"Shake it up, Stud," you holler out the window when you're back up on your throne. "Come on, boy, throw them wires aboard. We're gonna make the quickest pickup in Monongahela history."

He tosses the wires over the tow knees and climbs aboard. You wiggle your stern out coming slow ahead. You back slow. When you're clear you come ahead and run down past the tipple to the lower end and make your turn and come up slow and then ring a stopping bell and drift up easy on your load. On the split second before you kiss the barge with a gentle thump you ring up a slow bell and it holds you against the barge while the deckhand dumps the face wires over the timberheads.

You jump down on deck again.

"Fly up and turn the head line loose!" you holler at the deckhand, who is standing there half dead.

You come ahead on the winches and even up your wires, and run back up to the pilothouse.

"*Don't* dream over it, boy!" you roar. "Come on back and turn the stern line loose. Run!"

He staggers back and turns loose and you come ahead slow and work your stern out because there's mud and rocks against the shore. And then you back and pull your rudders down the opposite way until that big load begins to swing and then bang! you come ahead and haul your rudders down the other way. The load is swinging now and you look back and check your stern.

Getting in pretty close astern, but we'll try it.

In a minute you're clear of everything and you're bound upriver and the tipple still stands there cold and dark and silent. No spectators, no cheering throngs to witness your brilliant feats.

You check the clock. A nine-minute landing. Even Duke could be proud of it.

"Get some lights out on that barge," you holler down into the darkness. "And tighten up on them wires a little."

Now everything is different again from the downtrip. The engine is working hard and you're edging upstream slow, three or three and a half miles an hour, you've got eight hundred tons now. You laugh out loud and think of the times you steered for pilots on the Mississippi, the Illinois, the Ohio—with eight, ten, twelve, fourteen thousand tons ahead of you.

The engineer comes back up. This is the good time, between three and five, when your heart's as big as the Allegheny Mountains and your spirits are like helium gas.

"You only rung ten bells on that landing," he says. "You must be feelin' good." He lights a cigarette.

"Did I ever tell you about the time," you say, "when we were in drydock down at Brownsville?"

"What was that?" he says.

"Duke was on vacation and old man Slater was on here as relief captain. We went into drydock with orders for new wheel, new rudders, new controls, new refrigeration, new generator, and some welding on leaks in the sponsons. So old Slater he put on his overalls and went to work with the crew on the repairs.

"He says to me, 'You give the boys a hand getting that generator out and the new one aboard.'

"I let that go in one ear and out the other and I went up and threw some stuff in the old suitcase and started up to the hotel. I figured two or three days in the hotel, a few hot baths and some time in the public library and I'd be about back to normal."

"How many loads the *Reliance* have?" says the engineer.

"Three," you reply. "Well, Slater meets me coming down the ladder and he says, 'Where you goin'?' 'Up to the hotel,' I says. 'Me for a hot tub. We got no plumbing, no heat, no nothing here. I can't see no future hanging around here for three days. Give me a call when we're ready to go.' He give me a funny look and he says, 'The company expects everybody on these here small boats to pitch in when the boat's in drydock. You're supposed to help out here.'

" 'Listen, cap,' I says, 'what do you reckon the pilot on the *Sprague* does when they're on the ways? You reckon he puts on an old pair of pants and gets into the wheel with a wrench?'

" 'No,' he says, 'he don't.'

" 'Well, how about the pilot on the *Jason*,' I says. 'Do you reckon he helps overhaul the pumps?'

" 'I don't s'pose he does,' says this mighty captain. 'But that's different.'

" 'What about the pilots on the *Homestead* and the *Vesta* and the *Charles Campbell* and the *Mongah* and the *Vulcan* and the *Slack Barrett* and the *Sam P. Suit* and the *Jack Rathbone* and the *Crucible* and the *Ernest Weir* and the *George T. Price* and the *Nicholas Duncan* and the *Sailor* and the *J. D. Ayres*—what do you imagine them pilots do while the boat is in drydock?'

" 'Why, I reckon they lay around uptown or go home until the work is done. But—'

" 'That's what I thought,' I says. 'And that's just what this pilot is gonna do right now. I hired out here as pilot and I work at it twelve hours a day. I ain't no deckhand, striker, engineer, captain, or welder's helper. Give me a call when you're ready to turn loose and go back to work. Good-bye.'"

"What did the company say?" says the engineer.

"Old Slater never said nothing to the company. He was all hot air. I knew he wouldn't and he didn't."

"Oh, if you want a taste of that you oughta be in the engine department. Why, down in the pools one time on the *Edgar Thomson* we broke the shaft and I was working day and night until I was so tired I could hardly crawl up to the sack. Meanwhile the deckhands was up the bank tearing the town apart. Oh, it's real glory to be an engineer. It's marvelous."

"My, didn't that old *Reliance* look nice tonight, though! You ever work on her?"

"I decked on her once when I was a kid. Captain Gilmore. Towing oil for Standard."

"She's about done, they say."

"All them old steamboats are about done. Twenty years and you'll go a long ways to hear a steam whistle here on the Mon or anyplace else."

"Oh, there'll be a few hang on."

"A damn few. Look at the crew they got to carry. Look at the upkeep. Why, with this old tub and a crew of eight we could shove those three she's got tonight, and I'll bet she's got twenty men aboard if she's got one. Oh, hell, they're done. Wheel repairs. Boiler trouble. Nothing but grief. Hard to handle. Licensed men. Rotten in the wind. Awkward around landings. They had their day."

"My, but they sure are pretty though."

"The inside of them boilers ain't pretty. Take it from one who's been in. And how long do you think it would of took you to make that pickup down at Rosedale with a big ole stern wheeler? Especially with a stiff wind blowing? Don't kid this boy. I spent fifteen years on them lousy steamboats. Fifteen years too long. You couldn't get me back on one of them babies, no, not for a chief's job."

"Oh, you're always taking the sour side of everything. They ain't as bad as all that."

"They're worse. How about some coffee?"

"Good idea. We're about done working for tonight. We'll get up to the lock and have an hour wait while the *Reliance* locks through. It'll be five-thirty by that time."

He goes away and you settle down and plan out the kind of house you're going to build someday and the barge line you're going to own, and you start thinking up names for the kids you're going to have and one way and another the night drags along. You lock through behind the *Reliance* and at five after six Duke shows up while you are spotting barges at Dupont. By now you are let down, tired, smoked too many cigarettes, and sick of it again.

"You get any sleep?" you say.

"Enough for a canary bird," he says. "I got her, kid."

"You got her," you say.

Another night watch on the Monongahela is over and you eat breakfast and go to bed, 6:30 A.M.

Chapter 20

World Without End

Well, then, it comes down to this. There are two kinds of men, those who live for appearances and comfort and those who live in a world of raw realities slugging their way to the graveyard proud, and sinking their teeth in life like it was Kansas City sirloin medium rare. The members of the group who go for Sunday afternoon drives with the kids and bowl on Thursdays can't for the life of them understand *how* the others ever busted loose. They know *why* well enough, but of course they won't even admit that much, the most of them. They talk as though they're perfectly satisfied with the squirrel-cage routine of life at the office and the Elks and, by God, pretty soon they *are* satisfied. Meanwhile cousin Slim, who "was always kinda harum-scarum," or brother Bill, who "was pretty erratic as a kid," is slogging the seven seas in rusty old tramp steamers, laying pipe line across the Persian sands, building bridges, booming oil in Manitoba, or, close to home, railroading or steamboating or pulling the transports across the plains, and sucking in a hundred dollars' worth of fresh air a minute. I guess it boils down to those who thrive on taking chances and those who turn pale at the thought. You'll never get past those city limits, boys, unless you just up and go.

"You look at them clerks in stores and all them guys like that that works inside," Duke used to say. "You'll notice you very seldom see a very old clerk or a bank teller. The life kills 'em off. No fresh air. Boss breathin' down their shirt collar all the time. Gotta keep them shoes shined. And the way they got to talk: 'We sincerely wish to congratulate youse on your highly influential deposit of four dollars and thirty cents net in your highly steamed account,' says the bank clerk. How would you like it, Beedle, to have to talk like that all day? After a few years you would be the stonecutter's delight."

"Another twelve months on here and they'll be giving a quantity discount on headstones for the lot of us," I said. We were all comfortable enough on the *Coal Queen* but that's the habit, talk it down, make it sound tough, build that romance, kid.

"But look here, Beedle, that's the beauty of it. *We* won't *be* here in twelve months most likely. We'll be on another boat with all new crew, new faces we never seen before, new stories we never heard, maybe on a new river, who knows? You never stand still in steamboatin', kid. But now take some of these uptown guys. Suppose you was short-order cook at the Rex Café—why, you'd be there an eternity before anything new come to pass."

"You picked a bum example," I said. "Them short-order cooks is worse boomers and roamers than steamboaters."

"Maybe so. But I'll bet you a good quart of Old Hickory that both you and me won't be here a year from today. You'll move on, kid, this here outfit ain't big enough for either you *or* me. Why, we're just kinda having a little scenic tour of the mountains. Pretty soon somethin' or other happen—boat burn up, company bust, get promoted, get disgusted, transfer, quit, or get fired. You never know what the next month has got on the order board for you, kid. That's why steamboatin beats the hell out of any other form of livin' that they have discovered up to now."

"My, you sound just like William Jennings Bryan," I said. "Only you're a lot prettier."

"You oughta see me on Saturday night," says Duke.

So the better element stay home and run the community and the wild ones that spent a lot of time up in the principal's office they buy a day-coach ticket and go someplace where they can holler out loud without somebody saying, "What'll that boy do next? It's a disgrace, that's what it is. Ohhhh, his poor mother."

When our high-spirited hero gets beyond the county line he may find right now that there are a lot of hard knocks that go with the romance; but to the disgust of the members of the "You'll-find-out" school of thought at home, who have been entertaining him with variations on this theme since he was old enough to button his own pants, the fugitive from Main Street or High Street or Water Street finds that the knocks are the best part of the game. After he gets a few he says to himself: Why, that ain't nothing like it was advertised. Give us some more.

So he gets a few more hard knocks and he thinks: This is the life. These here knocks are just pie. They make me feel mighty lively and friendly.

"Brother," says an old deckhand to me once in a saloon down at Homestead, Pa., "why, if you think deckin' here in the pools is work you oughta been along with me in the days of the Combine. Workin' them old spring pole pumps in the rain and snow. Wheelin' coal. Carryin' them 27-foot chains. And quarters! Why, hell, we never knew what a bunk was like. We just laid down on the deck wherever we could find a place. They use to throw the food out in tin panikins and we scrambled for it. Misery —why, man, it was nothin' else clear through."

"I wouldn't work on no boat like that," I said, swallowing some Iron City beer.

"We was used to it," he said. "It wasn't so bad."

Hard knocks? Well, I imagine Lewis and Clark and Daniel Boone and General Zebulon Pike and Captain Shreve and old Christopher Columbus himself had enough hard knocks to go around, but they "was used to it" and they were following some distant banner in the sky that other people couldn't see or didn't care about. After they and their gang, the pioneers, had gone ahead and got all the hard knocks and cleared the way the others followed along, stepping pretty gingerly, carrying their guns on the half-cock, and complaining about the plumbing and the food. Nowadays the frontiers are gone, so the pioneer type go off to sea or to the oilfields, or railroading, or they take to the river and get slammed around so bad it would discourage a normal person. But they're not like other people. They don't mind being slammed around—it gives them a chance to slam right back. Which is what they want, what they thrive on.

You meet all kinds out on the river. On the Monongahela you meet Italians and Poles, and Hungarians and Germans and I don't know what all. Up the Illinois you work with boys from the slums of Chicago and farm boys off the Illinois black dirt country. Up on the Mississippi you meet great-grandsons of the Iowa pioneers, and Swedes and Norwegians from the big northwest country. Down on the Lower Mississippi you're working alongside of Cajuns, who talk a funny lingo, and rough boys from Memphis or New Orleans, who speak with slow and quiet voices. And all this mighty crew of rivermen gang together, they are a breed, like railroaders. Oh, they're not all bold and reckless adventurers—a heap of them are as dumb and drab and spiritless as can be, but in the main they want to go places and do big things out under the sky.

And when the steamboat whistles blow, they put down the beer glass, grab their gauntlet gloves and caps, and go down the bank again and climb onto some old river boat.

And when the whistle blows and they have to get out and make a lock they cuss and moan and claim they're gonna quit. But mostly they stay. That's the way it always was on the river, and the way it always will be, until the Monongahela and the Youghiogheny and the Tygart and the West Branch run dry, and the last steamboat whistle has echoed back off the hills, filling the valleys with that mournful music that haunts you wherever you go.

Acknowledgments

A great part of this book was written in the peaceful back room of the Carnegie-Stout Public Library in Dubuque, and I want to thank all the girls of the library staff for their kind co-operation, especially Miss Elsie Datisman for her efforts in getting rare books for me from various eastern libraries.

Captain Frederick Way, Jr., of Sewickley, Pa., and Captain Donald Wright, editor of the *Waterways Journal* of St. Louis helped me whenever I ran aground and I am grateful for their assistance, and also for their generosity in permitting quotations from their works.

For good reasons I am also indebted to Bernard De Voto, A. J. Brosius of the Union Barge Line, Kenny Sheffler of the Central Barge Company, and Bernard Bergman of National Distillers Corporation, Philadelphia.

Thanks to my dad for the use of his library, and for procuring me a copy of *The Navigator*, priceless sourcebook on the western rivers.

More than thanks to Marian Van Patten Bissell for sound editorial help, typing and proofreading drudgery, and consistent morale building without which I would never have quit whittling and started writing.

Bibliography

There must be hundreds of books written about the Monongahela. I'm not a scholar, so I don't pretend that this list is anything but a guide to *some* of the most interesting material about the river and the region.

ALBIG, W. ESPEY. *Early Development of Transportation on the Monongahela River*. Ohio Valley Historical Association Report, 1914. v. 8: 66-74.

AMBLER, CHARLES HENRY. *A History of Transportation in the Ohio Valley*. Glendale, Calif.: Arthur H. Clark Co., 1932.

CALLAHAN, JAMES MORTON. *History of the Making of Morgantown, West Virginia: A Type Study in Trans-Appalachian Local History*. Morgantown, W. Va., 1926.

CRAIG, NEVILLE B. *The History of Pittsburgh*. Pittsburgh: John H. Mellor, 1851.

CRAMER, ZADOK. *The Navigator*. Pittsburgh: Cramer, Spear and Eichbaum, 1817.

DRAVO CORPORATION. *Locks and Dams*. Pittsburgh, 1947.

DUNBAR, SEYMOUR. *A History of Travel in America*. New York: Tudor Publishing Co., 1937.

Early Western Travels, 1748–1846. (A. Michaux, F. A. Michaux, T. M. Harris.) Cleveland: Arthur H. Clark Co., 1904.

FREEMAN, DOUGLAS SOUTHALL. *George Washington*. New York: Charles Scribner's Sons, 1948.

Frontier Defense on the Upper Ohio. Compiled from the Draper manuscripts in the library of the Wisconsin Historical Society. Madison, 1912.

GIPSON, LAWRENCE HENRY. *The British Empire Before the American Revolution.* Volumes IV, VI, VII. New York: Alfred A. Knopf, 1946.

GOULD, *Fifty Years on the Mississippi, or Gould's History of River Navigation.* Nixon-Jones Printing Co., 1889. (A fine facsimile edition of this excellent book has just been published by Longs College Book Store, Cincinnati.)

HULBERT, ARCHER BUTLER. *Braddocks Road and Three Relative Papers.* Cleveland: Arthur H. Clark Co., 1903.

————. *The Old Glade (Forbes') Road.* Cleveland: Arthur H. Clark Co., 1903.

HUNTER, LOUIS C. *Steamboats on the Western Rivers.* Cambridge: Harvard University Press, 1949.

LATROBE, JOHN B. H. *The First Steamboat Voyage on the Western Waters.* Baltimore, 1871.

Light List, Mississippi and Ohio Rivers and Tributaries. Washington, D. C.: U.S. Government Printing Office.

LILLARD, RICHARD G. *The Great Forest.* New York: Alfred Knopf, 1947.

Lloyd's Steamboat Directory and Disasters on the Western Waters. Cincinnati: James T. Lloyd & Co., 1856.

MANTE, THOMAS. *History of the Late War in North America, and the Islands of the West Indies.* London: W. Strahan and T. Cadell, 1772.

MAXIMILIAN, PRINCE OF WIED. *Travels in the Interior of North America.* Cleveland: Arthur H. Clark Co., 1905.

Monongahela River Navigation Charts. The District Engineer, Pittsburgh District. Pittsburgh, Pa.

MORRISON, JOHN H. *History of American Steam Navigation.* New York: W. F. Sametz and Co., 1903.

Pennsylvania. American Guide Series. New York: Oxford University Press, 1946.

VEECH, JAMES. *The Monongahela of Old.* Privately Printed. Pittsburgh, 1892.

WAY, CAPTAIN FREDERICK JR. *Towboats Old and New.*
Sewickley, Pa.: Steamboat Photo Co., 1946.
———. *Inland River Record.* Sewickley, Pa., 1950.
West Virginia. American Guide Series. New York: Oxford
University Press, 1946.
WILEY, RICHARD T. *Monongahela,—The River and Its Region.*
Butler, Pa.: Ziegler Co., 1937.

INDEX